PERSONAL POWER

FROM PASSENGER TO PILOT

28 SIMPLE STRATEGIES TO RECLAIM HAPPINESS & LIVE <u>YOUR</u> LIFE

BY LUCY DAY
"THE MODERN MEDIUM"

First Published in Australia by

Light Path Press, October 2015

Copyright © 2015 by Lucy A. Day

themodernmedium.com

The moral rights of the author have been asserted.

All rights reserved. No part of this book may be used or reproduced by any mechanical, photographic or electronic process, or in the form of a phonographic recording; nor may it be stored in a retrieval system, transmitted or otherwise be copied for public or private use, other than for 'fair use' as brief quotations embodied in articles and reviews, without prior written permission of the publisher.

The information given in this book should not be treated as a substitute for professional advice; always consult a specialist. Any use of information in this book is at the reader's discretion and risk. Neither the author nor the publisher can be held responsible for any loss, claim or damage arising out of the use, or misuse, or the suggestions made or the failure to take professional, specialist advice.

Cover design by **hellopants.com.au**

To my husband and Co-Pilot

Thank you for giving me both roots and wings

Contents

Introduction	5
What is Personal Power?	9
Sink or Swim	11
Keep it Simple, Stupid	17
Power starts from the Inside	23
Learn how to love	33
Shit Happens	39
Who's the victim?	49
Acceptance is Beautiful	55
Create Change	61
Forgive yourself	71
Take Responsibility	79
Look inside for Answers	85
Choose your fights Wisely	93
Become Decisive	99
Aim High	105
Stop Complaining	111
Drop the concept of Perfection	117

Be Honest	125
Live in the Moment	131
Learn to Let Go	139
Focus on Respect	145
Leave the Competition	151
Turn your back on Drama	159
Give More than you Receive	163
Forgive Others	169
Choose your Friends Wisely	177
Choose the right path	183
Be fearless	187
Count your blessings	195
Fake it	201
Time for Take off	205
About the Author	207
Thank you!	209
Your Invitation to The Flight School	211
Praise for Lucy Day	213

Introduction

As a psychic medium and life coach, I spend my working life inside the lives of some beautiful souls. In fact everyone I have met has had beauty, love, light and passion at their core. Sure, they may not lead perfect lives, may have made a few questionable choices, lost track of life a little, even hurt and been hurt along the way. But truly, if you could see the goodness that resides in each of us, you'd know why I am so passionate about helping everyone to achieve peace and happiness. All any of us truly want is to love and be loved. That's it. You're all bloody beautiful inside. I just wish you could see it.

Most of my clients have suffered from a crisis of confidence at some point in their lives, as have I, and have found themselves paralysed by fear — of the past repeating itself, of making a mistake or simply of what might or might not happen if they dare to change. We all have desires, ambitions and wishes for our lives, yet many of us are unable to move forward into the future we deserve because we're chained by sad memories and experiences of the past.

We are all born with an equal ability to have a wonderful life. Of course we all have different backgrounds, talents, interests, skills and ambitions, which means that our paths are very different. But there is no reason why each and every one of us can't be happy and successful in our own way.

However life is no garden full of roses. I believe we are here to learn and grow and develop, not just as humans but also as souls, so we face numerous tasks, choices and difficulties in order to test our strength, evolve spiritually and teach us more about ourselves. How we deal with these lessons will dictate whether we have to keep repeating the same lesson or we move on having grown and empowered ourselves.

Having dealt with difficult situations in my own life and helped others to work through theirs, I fully believe that the trick to getting on in life is hidden in how we manage our personal power and how we align with our true purpose, how honest we are with ourselves and how well we make our decisions in line with this.

Our journey through life takes many unexpected turns and it is often then that we seek outward guidance, a reassurance that everything will be ok.

Clients often tell me they simply want to be happy, to have peace of mind — my response? 'Take your power back' and then I work on seeing how that applies to them as individuals.

In my own life, when I struggle with a situation or feel worried about something, I stop and remind myself that I'm giving my power away. Simply acknowledging this starts an internal dialogue and then, using the strategies in this book, which work every single time, I have a solution to my concerns and instantly change my perspective from helpless to empowered.

As much as I enjoy seeing my clients' potential futures, when someone in need of reassurance comes to see me, I have always been guided to give more than just predictions. The momentary joy felt by a client who hears 'all will be fine' is often heavily outweighed by the reality of returning home to their problems and wondering 'But how?' and 'When?'

As much as we like to know what's going to happen – for it takes away the fear of the unknown - when you simply tell someone the future you see for them, you replace potential action with hope and remove any personal responsibility. You take away their personal power.

Throughout this book, just as in my private readings, I will help you to see your present situation more clearly, release the shadows of your past, and present, and empower you to create a happy future for yourself. This, I believe, is worth far more than giving away empty promises of what 'might be'.

This is a book about you - your journey, your transformation - your access to your true self. During this journey, I will transform you from the passenger of your life to the pilot.

Every chapter has a 'Power Up Practice' with thought provoking and empowering activities for you to do. You may be asked to write down your thoughts, read a story or answer a few simple questions that will quickly dig deep into your soul.

I hope you enjoy the diary aspect to your journey, and rather than just read the words, allow them to work on you, to imprint your soul and ignite your soul. Then, one day, when you have long since transformed into the pilot of your life, you may well pick up this book and see how far you have come. There is nothing like observing your growth to feel a sense of self-pride and accomplishment.

I've split the process up into 28 'power up' strategies, each one powerful on its own. The concepts are really pretty simple in their essence — for the best advice in life is always simple and never complicated. However, it's not just 'knowing' that will help you to regain your personal power, it's doing, being, living, absorbing and understanding.

Enjoy your journey into your own self, taking back your personal power and determining a future that you alone desire.

Never apologise for being you. You are already perfect in your own imperfect way.

It's time to take your personal power back…

Lucy

What is Personal Power?

Wars have been fought, blood has shed, cities destroyed, nations obliterated. All because of power struggles between world leaders. But these power struggles are played out in full view of the world; angry, brutal and obvious.

By contrast, Personal Power is so subtle, so unspoken, so undefined, that most of us don't know we've got it until it's gone.

It is, quite simply, the power you have over your life.

If you've ever felt overwhelmed, frustrated or stuck; if you've avoided something or someone; felt helpless in the face of adversity; blamed someone else for your unhappiness, or simply felt like life has been passing you by, then you know what it's like to have given away your personal power.

Giving away personal power is completely disabling. Without it, we can't be ourselves, do what we want to do, enjoy the life we deserve or truly live our lives. Personal power is the lifeblood of our soul.

But no matter how important it is, we give it away with such ease, without knowing its true value. We are told as children to stand up for ourselves, be brave, be proud, have confidence, but we are never taught to keep hold of our personal power. It's like a hidden secret weapon that no one realises we have inside each and every one of us.

Success is not the key to happiness. Happiness is the key to success

Albert Schweitzer

Giving away your personal power is like putting the light out on your potential happiness. I could have said success, but at the end of the day, what you really want is to be happy, right? You could be successful and completely miserable — because success is so subjective. One person's idea of success is completely different to another's. But happiness, well that's the Holy Grail. You could be happy with nothing material to your name, but with peace in your heart and love at your side.

If you want a book that tells you what the perfect life looks like, this isn't it. Such a book doesn't exist. I can't create it for you or tell you how it looks, but I can give you the tools to build it yourself. And you know what, contentment tastes far sweeter when you've achieved it for yourself and composed it according to your tastes, desires and dreams.

When you know you've not had to rely on anyone else for your inner peace, now that is REAL success.

Sink or Swim

"I had two choices. To get on with what was left of my life, or to lie there and give up. Giving up would have been a long and lonely route, so I chose the other. I got up and got on with it..."

Jamie, a good friend of mine, was diving into the cooling water of the River Thames one hot and sunny Sunday morning in 2004, with a group of friends. They had taken a picnic with them and after having something to eat, they all decided to go back into the water in the late afternoon. Jamie went back to the same spot that he had been diving off earlier in the day and dived into the river.

What he didn't know at the time is that the River Thames is tidal and in the time it had taken them to eat their lunch, the level of the water had changed substantially. As Jamie plunged into the now shallow water, his head collided with a large rock, compressing his spinal column and, as he later found out, breaking his neck.

Jamie had been a very active guy. At only 25 years old, he lived with his girlfriend in a top floor flat. He was a keen mountain climber, loved riding his bike and running and was a newly qualified doctor of chiropractic. He had a very active social life, loved skiing holidays, trekking, mountaineering and travelling. Basically his whole life revolved around being outdoors, being active, energetic and busy.

A few days after his accident, Jamie woke up out of the induced coma he had been in, to be told that he had two collapsed lungs and was paralysed from the neck down. His prognosis was poor; he would certainly never walk again and would need specialist care for the rest of his life. He had no movement in his hands, no triceps strength, which meant he would need an electric wheelchair to get around, and he felt nothing from his chest down. Doctors confirmed there was nothing that could be done to remove his paralysis.

Faced with this level of adversity, it is easy to assume how you would feel in Jamie's situation. To be trapped in a paralysed body would be so difficult to handle. How you possibly live any sort of life? Every waking day would be so damn hard to get through, surely?

However, from that day, Jamie did something that even now, ten years later, I find amazing.

He never stopped smiling.

As we, his friends and family, visited him in hospital and later in rehab, our hearts broke to see our once active, healthy friend lying in a hospital bed, his muscles effectively wasting away. He was physically shrinking before our eyes and without fail we would hold our tears until we left his room, when the floodgates would open.

Little did we know that even though his physical body was shrinking, his mental strength was growing at a rate of knots.

He never had anything but a smile for us. He honestly never complained. He worked as hard as he could to get through the gruelling rehab so he could go home. Within six months, he had booked a holiday to South

America with his girlfriend and his caregiver. Only nine months after his accident, his medical team determined he was well enough to go on the trip. In fact it went so well that on his return he booked a further trip to Australia to visit some friends. He knew no bounds. Nothing was going to stop him, paralysed or not.

During his rehab, he was told that he should consider suing the Thames Council, as there were no signs warning of the tides and rocks. Jamie's response was that it was his responsibility, for he had chosen to jump into the water and that it was an accident. He kept the blame firmly at his own door.

He then had to move back to his native Sweden because he could no longer sustain the flat he had previously paid for with his salary. As a non-UK permanent resident, he had no rights to any disability benefit or assistance. Instead of bemoaning the fact, he enrolled himself in university to study as a psychologist – a job he knew didn't have any physical requirements, just his brain. In this way, he ensured that he could earn money and pay his way through life; something he had always intended on doing before his accident.

A few years later, he proposed to the girlfriend who had stayed with him throughout his recovery. He didn't go down on one knee to propose, nor did he get to walk down the aisle; he did things his way, his new way.

Despite being told that they may never be able to conceive, they now have two beautiful children.

Jamie's story is the perfect illustration of someone who kept a tight hold on his Personal Power against all the odds. He didn't blame anyone else for his predicament. He accepted his situation straight away, rather than wasting time and energy fighting what he couldn't change. He did what he could with a difficult situation and not for one second did he become a victim of his circumstances.

You might say that Jamie is a one-off, a special kind of person to be able to cope with all that in such an amazing way, but you know what? He's just a person, like the rest of us. He just chose to embrace a can do attitude and took his Personal Power back.

Fortune favours the brave, not the victim. I will show you how to break out of the confines of victim status and reclaim your future. Get the life you want, need and deserve; transform your routine of complaints and excuses into one of joy and gratitude.

Taking back your power is like taking the lead on the flight of your life — choosing to step out of the passenger seat and becoming the pilot. Taking responsibility for the destination and for all the joy, excitement and happiness that you experience during the ride.

When you gather up your personal power, you stop blaming others for your lack of happiness, you release fear and empower yourself to live a fearless life, without limits. You are no different to anyone else! You too can have the life you want.

The journey begins here...

life is really simple, but we insist on making it complicated.

- Confucius

Keep it Simple, Stupid

If you look back, you'll feel that life seemed so much easier when you were a child. But you know, the truth is, life still has the potential to be easy. The difference is that as we get older, we make things far more complicated for ourselves.

As young children, we see life as a box of chocolates waiting to be opened. We have little concept of self-doubt or questioning, we have no hidden agendas, no hang-ups, irrational fears or painful pasts dragging us down. We simply see life for the hope and excitement it offers.

As toddlers we judged people in simple terms; if they smiled, we smiled back — we liked them. If they looked sad or grumpy, we kept away. We ate when we wanted to, slept when we needed to and played to our hearts content. We fell over and got straight back up again. We tried something a hundred times before we got it right, with a few tantrums along the way, but in the end we did it. There was nothing but the here and now. No fears for the future, no hang ups about the past.

Sure, as adults we have responsibilities, we can't just play, sleep and eat all day, like we did as children. But every single one of us allows our minds to become negatively affected by difficult experiences. We start to doubt ourselves and stop listening to our intuition. We question our instincts and avoid anything that seems too hard, before even trying.

Rather than communicate our worries, we bottle them up, some of us turning to external influences for a release — alcohol, drugs, partying, comfort eating and more. We learn to manipulate people to get what we want, can hold grudges against people who have hurt us and may avoid others who have similar traits in case they hurt us too. We can lie not only to others, but also to ourselves, ignoring our conscience and turning our back on our morals, taking the attitude that 'everyone else is doing it, so I may as well too'.

And before we know it, we have made our lives more and more complex, losing sight of who we are and what we really need to be happy.

We create responsibilities, desires, needs and wants, which result in hang-ups, disappointments, regrets and worries. Our financial burdens can be complicated enough before we even start on emotional ties.

Boredom is a great trigger of complication. Our lives may feel a bit dull, facing the same old routines every day, getting nowhere, just existing, and so we start to jazz things up a bit. We introduce lots of new goals and plans which all come with their own 'issues'. These reactive, short-term decisions then create massive overwhelm: 'what the heck have I done? My life was so much easier before and now I'm in a mess!'

Being busy must not be confused with being useful. By living more simply, you can become far more efficient and effective and achieve far more than if you try to handle lots of things at once.

By living a complicated life, you send your personal power off in so many different directions that it's no wonder you feel helpless and unable to move forward, bound by the past. Decisions become impossible because so many things ride on them, so many parts of your life are bound by each other.

Complicated lives send us off into negative thinking patterns and our personal power becomes trapped by our concerns. We worry about our past mistakes or current problems, and what might happen in the future. The only time we ever seem to stop thinking is when we're asleep; otherwise our minds are a constant whirlwind. Most of the thinking we do is completely pointless, eventuating in nothing more than worries and concerns, stress and mental fatigue. How many times a day would you say that your thinking is constructive? It's more likely that you are really just thinking yourself into confusion and negativity.

When life feels complicated, remember this: there is a solution to every problem; nothing is impossible. So let's start unravelling this tangled life of yours. I'm not going to start delving into your past, for what would be the point of that? Dragging everything that has hurt you back into the present so it can hurt you again? No thank you. We are going to start with detangling the here and now — today.

In simplicity is real power.

Think of the most influential or life-changing things you have ever heard or read — I will bet that they have been so simple, yet so impactful. That's because great things, actions, people and practices don't have to be complicated, they just have to connect.

By simplifying our lives, we create instant power, instant self-control. We feel lighter and less burdened, we have more space and time for creativity, for connection to our tasks and to others. We have space to enjoy life, to do the things that make our soul happy. We have time for progression, growth and understanding. We give ourselves a much-needed break!

Whether you feel life has spiralled out of control or you have willed it into something more complicated, over the next few chapters we will snap your personal power back and simplify your life, making it easier to navigate, bringing more peace to your day and night and allowing you space to breathe, think constructively and create YOUR best life.

POWER UP PRACTICE

Let's start with an affirmation: write the affirmation below down on a piece of paper and stick it to the fridge. Repeat this in your head or out loud every time you pass or open the fridge...

In the coming chapters we will break down all the areas of your life that make it far more complicated than it needs to be. But for today, keep it very simple and just repeat the affirmation above. The process of reclaiming your personal power is a simple one, so we start as we mean to go on.

be gentle
first with
yourself
if you wish
to be gentle
with others...

- Lama Yeshe

Power starts from the Inside

- BE GOOD TO YOURSELF -

If we knew we had to have the same car for the rest of our lives, we would make sure it was regularly serviced and that we used the best parts and fuel that we could afford. We would keep it clean and tidy and make sure the rust and rot didn't set in. We would care for that car and ensure that it lasted forever.

Funny then how most of us, despite knowing that we only have one mind and one body for the rest of our lives, treat it like a car we can dispose of whenever we fancy a new one.

We don't think about what we eat, we work ourselves into exhaustion, stress our minds into depression and confusion and generally use and abuse the only body we have.

Yes, we can go to the hospital and get ourselves fixed up to a degree, but that's like crashing the car constantly and going to the body shop on a regular basis for new panels and repair. It's hard getting around in a car with lots of problems that breaks down on you constantly and limps around town.

The body is an amazing system, designed to withstand some real abuse and carry us for what really is a very long time. Yet we are often amazed when something goes wrong and we get sick or suffer from disease. The fact is that unless we look after ourselves, we are fast-forwarding into pain and illness, whether that's mental or physical.

When it comes to personal power, it starts at the very source of ourselves – within our energy systems. Our body is made up of energy and therefore it stands to reason that if we don't control what energy (food, etc.) goes in, then we can't control what that energy is transformed into (weight gain, disease, discomfort). Our personal power escapes our grasp and moves into the food we consume, the guilt we have for eating the wrong things or not exercising or the diseases and illnesses we get.

Of course not all disease is caused by poor self-management but we can make massive positive contributions to our health by taking care of ourselves.

It has become the norm to associate guilt with what we eat, to chastise ourselves for eating too much or too little, to associate eating with depression and worry, to gorge or starve and then feel terrible about it afterwards.

Food has an immense strength when it comes to taking away our personal power. Not only can a cream cake crush willpower in a second, but also the energy that we give simply to thinking about food, both positively and negatively, can be overwhelming.

Yet, food is a wonderful, plentiful resource where we live. We are so lucky to have the choices we have and the abundant fresh produce from local sources and shipped in from around the world. The creativity that comes with making delicious, healthy dishes and the satisfaction you feel when you eat something nutritious and tasty is a gift. We're also incredibly lucky because healthy food doesn't mean nasty-tasting anymore.

This isn't a book about how to lose weight or what foods to eat; goodness knows there are plenty of resources for helping yourself on that positive path. But I cannot stress enough how important what you eat is, if you want to retain personal power. If you have a negative relationship with food, you give away personal power at the very source.

Not only what you eat but also the type of thought process that surrounds eating will have a huge effect on your personal power. If you select a microwave meal in a rush, consume it out of guilt and then spend an evening regretting it, the whole process has been negative and you have literally spent hours giving power to that one meal.

So, it stands to reason that if we eat foods that taste healthy, we can choose them using a positive thought process, eat them with a saintly glow and feel pretty much guilt-free.

Lisa came to see me at my office for a reading. She had a number of personal issues which all centred on her relationship, career and finances. Lisa was holding herself back from finding happiness because she projected her past experiences into her perceived future — she fully believed that because she'd had what she felt was a tough life up until now, that was all she could expect from the future.

As I linked to Lisa's energy, her Grandmother came through and started wagging her finger at Lisa. She showed me images of Lisa sitting on her sofa at home, eating chocolate and cakes and drinking wine. Now, we all do this from time to time, but she showed me that this was Lisa's only pleasure in life. Lisa then showed me energetically the guilt and regret that followed her binge sessions and the heaviness in her stomach and hips.

As I scanned her, I could feel a blockage in the energetic centre around her tummy, which we call the Solar Plexus. The Solar Plexus is linked to will power, personal power, confidence, responsibility and reliability. I felt that she was hugely depleted in this area and that the empty feeling was manifested in Lisa as an uncontrollable hunger.

Thus Lisa never seemed to feel full. So she ate and ate, putting on weight and in turn feeling more and more unhappy with her appearance, lack of physicality, lack of energy and impetus to exercise and, more recently, to walk further than to her car and back.

Gaining weight, losing her sense of identity and feeling guilty in turn made her not like herself very much. She hated her appearance and felt guilty about her extra weight. The spiral of feeling out of control in her outer life had taken on a life of its own, affecting her mentally, physically, emotionally and energetically.

Lisa and I worked on ways to get her moving again, but I knew that we needed to find out who she really was behind all the negativity. So I worked on redefining her identity and reason for being, kick started her willpower and showed her how to take back her personal power and work on her confidence. By finding the route of the problem she could then work to make her relationship with food a positive one.

When you look at yourself in the mirror, what do you see? Do you count your imperfections before covering them up with makeup, or do you have as quick a glance as you can to avoid seeing any more of what disappoints you?

Chances are that you hardly ever truly like what you see, for we are all so very obsessed by our looks nowadays that we have been taught to find fault with ourselves. It's no wonder really, since those in the media have done such a great job of convincing us all that anything less than perfection is ugly.

Every time we criticize our face, our body, our weight, we allow a little piece of personal power to ebb away from us.

Even if you can't flick a switch to like what you see, you can certainly teach yourself to shift your focus from the negative to the positive.

See those crow's feet spanning out from your eyes? They used to be known as 'laughter lines' before someone in the media likened them to crows' feet. Laughter lines show you've lived, they are literally memories of how many times your life has made you happy.

What about those lines around your lips? Memories of every kiss you have puckered up for and planted on a loved one.

Your face is your legacy, a map of where you have lived and loved. Sure, it may not be as young and relaxed as it once was, but you've lived! Without the ageing, you wouldn't have the experience of life you now have. Do you really want to go back to being 15 and do it all again?

If you choose to make positive changes to your appearance, well go ahead and do what you need to do to feel content, but in the meantime, be kind to yourself. You only have one body and it has been kind to you. It's only aged in the way it was always going to naturally do and you are just as beautiful as you ever were — beauty shines out of you like a beacon.

Don't give power to the parts of your appearance that you don't like. When you start to feel self-conscious and unattractive, you'll find you want to go out less, your confidence will be affected and you won't be yourself. Take the power back from your negative self-image— take control of those nasty thoughts and start seeing the beauty in you.

We wouldn't put a baby to sleep in a dirty cardboard box, but many of us reside in homes that metaphorically resemble little more than that. So many clients come to see me with the energy that they really dislike where they live, some even avoid going home from work until it's late enough to go straight to bed.

It's a basic human need to feel safe and secure in our homes. If you know that you live in a relatively safe neighborhood, then security in your home is pretty much covered so you then move onto wanting comfort, peace and pleasure from your home environment.

Sure, we don't all live in the homes of our dreams, but then we often have much higher expectations and tastes than our finances allow. It is entirely possible to make a home out of anywhere that you live.

Take the power away from your surroundings, stop them from keeping you from happiness. Don't allow those four walls to drag you down! Turn your discontent into gratitude to yourself for the fact you have a home at all and then kick start your creativity and make your home somewhere you want to be.

For some, a house can contain sad memories, in which case a complete change around of furniture, some new colours on the walls and a reshuffle of decorations can made a huge difference for now. Perhaps then a move to a new house with fresh opportunity would make for a positive future plan.

For others, the house may be rented and not feel like yours, or give you the feeling of stability you require, in which case, it is time to refocus your expectations. If you are in a position to purchase in the future, then make this a goal and focus your attentions on how to achieve this financially and practically. Remember however that even though the house you live in right now may not have your name on the mortgage, it is still your home. It's where you lay your head at night and where you make memories—where your life is taking place. Be grateful to yourself for what you have—a roof over your head, somewhere to be safe, warm, to eat and relax. This is YOUR home. Maybe one day you will have a mortgage with your name on it, maybe not—only you can make that happen. Take your power back by remembering that having a mortgage is not a prerequisite for happiness. Your happiness is dictated by how you perceive what you have right now, not by what you may or may not have in the future.

Quite simply, if you don't like it, don't fight it or avoid it — change your thinking, change your situation, improve your outlook or move away from it. Do something.

A cluttered home means a cluttered mind, and a loss of personal power to inanimate objects. It's so stifling to be surrounded by clutter. There's more to tidy up, to worry about, to clean around and sort though and that's if you're motivated to do so! Not to mention the guilt we have at having a house full of things we don't use and in many instances don't even like any more. The time it takes to find something in a cluttered house, drawer or wardrobe just increases your feeling of overwhelm, frustration and powerlessness.

If your house is a bit of a mess, don't worry, you're in good company. There are very few people who have a tidy house all of the time. But this isn't about a bit of mess, this is about simplifying, clearing and making space in your home and your mind.

If there is a room in your house which you know is unruly and secretly drives you mad, this is the missing source of your power!

A clear space is like a blank canvas, available to be used to create something great. Getting truly organised and clutter-free can vastly improve your daily life and it's such a simple start to take your power back.

Yes, even inanimate objects take our personal power and control us far more than we realise. People who are intensely tidy, for example, can attempt to take control of their lives by becoming obsessive about having everything tidy and in its right place. This attempt to gain power over the self by being so structured and controlled actually lends itself to the ultimate loss of personal power. Ironically, the more obsessed someone is with having everything 'just so' the more they give their power over to order. In this sense, personal power is actually gained by learning to relax and let go.

At the very source of our being, there are so many ways we can lose ultimate personal power.

By taking steps to take care of our bodies, our homes and our personal spaces, we are instantly taking care of our energy and bringing our power back to the core. When we have our personal power back, we are strengthened, energized and motivated to go and create our ideal life.

With our personal power in tact, we let nothing stop us, we move forward with ease and confidence, with contentment and peace in our hearts. We are independent, in charge and in control.

POWER UP PRACTICE

Pick a day one weekend and go into your 'room of doom' (aka the cluttered minefield that has been driving you mad) with some bin bags and get organising. Quickly review every item —'Does it give you joy? Do you look forward to wearing it or using it?' If the answer is yes, a real yes, then keep. It not, get rid of it!

Remember that every item in your home has been purchased with hard earned money – yours or someone else's. Next time you dump something on the floor, remember the joy it gave you when you purchased it or received it. Have respect for your efforts, your purchases and your gifts. They may not give you the same joy or excitement now but they once did and they cost you energy, in the form of money. Bring value back into your possessions.

With gratitude in your heart, be BRAVE, be BOLD and RELEASE anything which doesn't serve you. Sell what you can, give the rest away to charity and then organize what's left. If you have a cluttered living or working space, it's instantly gratifying and empowering when you put some time into clearing it up. Try to organise as you re-stock your cupboards and shelves. Google 'folding tips' for great ideas on how to get more into small spaces.

Clearing is addictive. Once you've done a room or area, you'll find that you want the whole house as tidy and easy to navigate. Little by little you will find yourself tackling a room, area or cupboard. Enjoy the process, it's hugely cathartic and your home will thank you for it. The less you have, the lighter your life!

dare to love yourself as if you were a rainbow with gold at both ends.

- Aberjhani

Learn how to love

- STARTING WITH YOURSELF -

'You've got to love yourself!' It's a phrase bandied around everywhere at the moment. 'Unless you love yourself, you will never be truly loved by anyone else!' But most of us find it really hard to state with conviction that we love ourselves. It just doesn't feel natural – it feels silly, like you're showing off, or being self-centred. So, because it doesn't feel right, we just don't do it, we avoid it.

There are far more of us open to admitting to self-loathing than self-loving. But when we actively dislike ourselves, we are really showing regret for our past actions and decisions or unhappiness with our looks or our bodies, for example. Some things we can change, others we were born with and have to learn to live with.

The power we give to the negative personal associations is intensely strong. Even an element of personal dissatisfaction is so disabling.

But self-love is the purest and the highest form of love. When you show yourself love, you automatically start appreciating and respecting yourself. If you have confidence and pride in what you do, you will begin to see yourself in a new light and be encouraged and inspired to do bigger and better things.

Unfortunately the old adage is true — how can someone else love you if you don't show yourself love? If you don't care for yourself it shows all over your face, in your body language, in your posture, in your energy. It comes out in the words you use to describe yourself.

The bottom line is, we need to learn to do it in one way or another!

Start simply — with acceptance. Sure, you've made some decisions along the way that haven't turned out to be the best. Yes, you have done things that you later regret. No, you're not a super model (but then there are only a handful on earth!) and yes, you could be a little more fit, healthy, kinder at times. But, you are you. There is only one of you and you are totally unique. When you accept who you are, warts and all, you go some way to taking responsibility for yourself and take your personal power back!

Acceptance precedes appreciation. You cannot appreciate yourself if you don't first accept who you are.

As the old mantra 'I love myself' feels strange to chant with any conviction, I find it so much easier to start by being grateful.

By appreciating the things that I have done for myself and my family, by appreciating the person that I am, I am showing myself that I'm not really that bad, that there are things to love. When I show myself gratitude, I am showing myself love, without shouting it for all and sundry to hear.

Chances are you don't care about yourself as much as you could. I meet people every day that are very harsh with themselves; self-critical and self-depreciating. I don't expect you to go from being your own harshest critic to a cheerleader overnight, but starting with appreciating what you've done for yourself over the years is a powerful start. Appreciating the physical body and what it has had to cope with is so important. We often take our body for granted until it starts to fall apart — the odd energetic boost in the form of a massage, energy healing or relaxation session can do wonders for keeping your energy up and balancing those roller coaster emotions.

The beauty of love is that it empowers you. When you see yourself with kind eyes, you give yourself confidence, courage, self respect, self esteem, all those key things that are drained, damaged when times become tough. If you go into difficult situations with a bank full of positive, powerful emotions like these, then you handle them better, you make better decisions, you operate with love and positivity in mind, rather than fear and negativity.

POWER UP PRACTICE

Imagine you're having a job interview and someone asks you to 'tell me three great things about yourself'.

Did you hesitate? Are you struggling to name the three things?

Now, imagine they ask you the same question about your best friend.

How quick is your response? Do you have a list of instant replies?

Chances are that yes, you do have more positive things to say about your best friend than yourself – because you value them and their attributes more than your own. Time to start seeing yourself in the same light. Be your own best friend.

Write an epitaph (the words that traditionally reside on a headstone in a graveyard) for yourself. What would you like it to say? How would you like to be remembered?

Your life is the story you leave behind and you're the star. Embrace everything about yourself and make your story worth telling.

The essential truth of life, he was coming to realize, wasn't romantic and took only two words to label:

shit. happens.

- J.R. Ward

Shit Happens

The world can be a difficult place. We all experience varying levels of heartbreak, pain, suffering, loss and tragedy, and being emotional creatures, these circumstances can take a lot out of us and put a negative cloud on our future outlook.

When the rug is pulled from under us, when life just comes and craps on us from above, it is normal to feel completely desperate, totally out of control and absolutely helpless.

Pain is part of our human experience so whatever you do don't lose faith in yourself. It may not feel like it at the time, but in suffering you will find great strength. When you look back at tragic times in your life, you will amaze yourself with what you have coped with and what you managed to get through. If you ever find yourself alone with a huge problem, see this as the ultimate test, to show you what you are made of. You have two options – sink or swim. So dig deeper than you ever knew you could and get paddling!

When you hit rock bottom, the only way is back up. At times like these, it's hard to know what to do, for the enormity of the problem can be so overwhelming it's paralysing.

When there truly seems to be no option in front of you, nothing you can do, do nothing. The answer will find its way to you. Don't rush. Positive, long term decisions are not made in a reactionary fashion, so give yourself a break. Accept that you are going to go through a range of emotions – disbelief, anger, fear, hopelessness and despair. Allow those emotions to flow through you but don't become those emotions. Let them go as quickly as they came. In time, you will find the strength to take back your power, embrace the change and make something positive out of this tough gig.

"All was seemingly right with the world and then one day, bang! My Boss took me into a meeting and handed me a redundancy letter. The worst of it was that I'd only been in the job for 3 months, so I only got a month's pay and had to leave there and then. I loved that job, it was really something I could get my teeth into, or so I thought. Not only that but because the pay was significantly more than I'd earned before, I had just signed a lease on a really expensive flat in town and had moved in only a few days earlier. With no job, I didn't know how I was going to keep my place.

I packed my few belongings up, went home and fell into a bottle of vodka, distractedly stared at the TV and wondered what the hell I was going to do.

It was about three weeks before I really got my head back into a space sensible enough to think straight. I literally spent those three weeks drinking the evenings away and feeling hopeless. But then one night, I watched a programme about business owners and I had a bit of a brainwave. My Dad had recently set up a law firm with a friend of his and although he had quite a few clients, I knew a lot more about social media and online advertising than he did. So, that night I ditched the bottle and wrote my Dad a basic proposal, outlining how I could potentially increase his customer base for very little cost, other than my time. I nearly deleted the document a few times but eventually decided that the only thing I could lose was my pride, if my Dad didn't go for it.

I expected him to turn me down, but when I sent it to him, he was really impressed. He offered me two months on a salary that would cover my flat and a few bills, to see if I could achieve what I'd said. He made it clear that I had one chance to prove myself to him and I wasn't getting any favouritism.

That was four years ago now, and I still work for my Dad's law firm, but I also have 16 other regular clients for whom I deliver marketing and sales to boost customer bases and income. My business is small, it's only me (and sometimes a freelancer when I'm busy) but it's successful and I absolutely love being my own boss.

I look back now and realise that I'd never have taken the plunge into self-employment had I not been made redundant. It was hitting financial rock bottom that made me look at my abilities differently and pretty much take a chance. It paid off."

Maxine, 34, London, U.K.

In tough times, you can find resilience, and in loss, you can find a renewed appreciation for life.

Sometimes we are vaguely aware that we want change, we need something different in our lives, but it's not until we are propelled into action that we are forced to see how much we needed that change and are made to do something about it.

Embrace change and realise it happens for a reason. It won't always be obvious at first, but one day you will look back and see the lesson. One of the most beautiful skills to learn in life is to be aware of and embrace the lesson as you are learning it, not in hindsight. When you are aware you are in the middle of a life lesson, you can harness the tools to get through it and the knowledge it is a lesson makes it somehow much easier to cope with.

There is always a reason. For everything that happens. Even if that reason is to learn empathy so that one day your story and your survival can help others. I know that my own suffering, my own story, has given me the empathy and understanding I need to help others. I can state with conviction that every insight I use to help my clients, has been one I have used to successfully overcome my own issues.

What you 'have' today may become what you 'once had' by tomorrow. You never know. Things change, often spontaneously. People and circumstances come and go. Life doesn't stop for anybody. It moves rapidly and rushes from calm to chaos in a matter of seconds.

Sometimes a single second in time changes the whole direction of our lives. Entire futures are flipped upside down, for better or worse, on the strength of an unpredictable event.

However challenging or fruitful a situation is now, it will change. That's the one thing you can count on. So when life is going well, enjoy it. Don't go looking for something better every second. Happiness never comes to those who don't appreciate what they have while they have it. In much the same way, remember that however tough life seems right now, this will change too. Nothing stays the same.

One of the toughest situations in life is the loss of a loved one. Grief is such a difficult emotion for anyone to process, even people in professions like me, who know that there is life after death and speak with 'the other side' every day! It's so hard to lose someone you love, to never have the chance to speak to them again, just to have their company, or to know they are there to turn to should you need them.

When it comes to grief, there are layers of progress which help you through the roller coaster of emotions, far too detailed for a single chapter in a book, but whether we progress through them with help or just allow ourselves to heal naturally, the process is the same.

There are two vital elements to dealing with tough times – one you can't control and one you can: time and acceptance.

Time heals all wounds. It's true. But time can be forever, or a split second. Remember that there is no normal, no expectation that you need to fall in line with. If it takes you forever to feel ok about your circumstances then so be it, it's your time, your timetable. If your heart has been hurt, for example, eventually, one day, the pain will feel less raw, the emotion inside you will have dropped lower than the surface and you will find that you can smile rather than cry. A day will come when you and your heart are ready to move on.

Acceptance of the situation, which is vital for us to move on, takes time too, but this is where your personal power comes into play. When you accept that life has taken a different turn and that your future will not be as you imagined, when you fully accept your change in circumstances, only then you can start to learn how to cope with your new life. Through acceptance, you take your power back from the realms of being a victim of the situation and take on your new reality in a position of strength. With acceptance, you are taking steps forward into your new beginning. With denial, you tie yourself to the past, to the 'what might have been', to regret, frustration and feeling completely stuck.

Remember that the future you feel you may have lost — what you 'thought' life would be like if only things hadn't changed — was only ever an illusion, created by your mind.

How it was 'supposed' to be all depends on what kind of thinker you are: if you're an optimist, chances are that you always imagine a future slightly brighter than the reality. As a pessimist, you may be someone who imagined only problems in the future.

If you were married, for example, and your relationship suddenly ended, you most likely would feel you had lost the plans and ideas for your future together. That is true. Life will be different, sadder, and lonelier at times. But think, how often has life ever turned out exactly like you imagined it anyway? You've coped with those unexpected turns and twists before. You've managed.

You managed then and you'll manage again now. How often have things just happened, cropped up out of the blue? That's the thing with life; it has an element of fate in that we start at A and finish at Z. But the roads we choose to get there will always surprise us with shock events. As much as we are in control of our personal fate to a degree, there are many situations beyond our control that can occur at any given point.

When tragedy strikes, change and deep trauma and upset are inevitable. Yes, it's a different future from what you were imagining. No, it's not the one you want or would have chosen, and possibly, if you could go back and change it, you would, even for a day. But when you accept that it is what it is, I mean really accept it, deep down into your soul, only then have you chosen to take control again and move forward in your own power.

When it comes to finding yourself in difficulty, there is a simple process you can recall to restore your power... Firstly, take a deep breath and remember that it will take time for you to truly accept the situation before you can take steps to remedy your emotions. This may take a few days, weeks or even months, depending on the gravity of the circumstances (and I can assure you that there are very few situations that you will find yourself in which are so grave that they takes months or years to accept).

Then remember that there is ALWAYS a way forward. There is ALWAYS a way out. Sometimes the only way out of a problem is to go straight through it, head down and eyes shut and hanging on for dear life. In whatever state you go, make sure the direction is forward.

When trouble occurs, our immediate response is to feel overwhelmed — 'what do I do? I can't cope!' We tend to spiral out of control by the end of the day, our helplessness peaking in the evening when we feel we truly cannot continue. So, do one thing — sleep on it.

Tomorrow is a new day and a fresh mind is far more useful to you than a troubled, tired one. Sleeping won't get rid of your problems but it will allow your mind to rest so you are working with a fresher perspective. Trying to solve your problems with a fatigued mind is like taking a strong sleeping pill and then going to the gym — one counteracts the other.

If you know you need help or support then *ask* for help. We are social creatures and people are more likely to want to help than we realise. It's natural to want to run and hide but thinking you should do it all alone is your ego taking over and self-punishment kicking in.

Talking is great therapy —sometimes just talking to a friend about how you feel helps you to brain dump. You don't always need to ask for someone else's advice; it's enough sometimes just to speak out loud, to get it out of your head. So share and put time and space around the issue. And remember...

There is ALWAYS a way forward.

Nothing is too hard for you to handle. Nothing. You will and can find a way through no matter how impossible it seems at the time. Have faith in yourself.

Yes shit happens, but so does sunshine. You have to know one to appreciate the other.

POWER UP PRACTICE

What do you fear the most?
....

How much control do you have over it happening?
....

Do you fully accept your current situation?
....

What are you 'pretending' doesn't exist, or isn't happening?
....

When did you last step out of your comfort zone? What happened?
....

Did you give in or overcome your fears?
....

If you could achieve one thing this year, what would it be?
....

→ Do one thing this week that feels uncomfortable, challenges your fears and puts you out of your comfort zone.

a wise woman wishes to be no one's enemy; a wise woman refuses to be anyone's victim.

- Maya Angelou

Who's the victim?

If you've ever heard yourself utter 'but it's not my fault' then truth is, in that situation, you've played the victim. There is a degree of personal responsibility in almost every negative oppressive emotion we attach to ourselves. Even if we have been the victim of a terrible crime that we feel was 100% not our fault, it is not the short term reaction to the crime that makes you a victim, it's the longer term response — how that changes you in the future, how you cope, to what extent you allow that one event to dictate the rest of your life.

Every day we read about soldiers returning from war zones with terrifying physical disabilities. Some go on to learn to cope with the changes to their bodies; others sink into depression and never truly 'live' again. A major difference between these soldiers is their mindset — their level of victim mentality. They are all victims of a war-related injury but not all choose to continue to be victims in the coming months and years when their attitude is vital to their recovery.

Continuing to align yourself with a victim mentality is the ultimate surrender of personal power. Whatever has happened in the past, allowing your present and future to be dictated by someone or something else, allowing them or it to control your happiness, is simply giving up. No matter how tough the situation you faced was, how awful or tragic the circumstances, becoming a victim of the situation is pure resignation from life.

Blame is one of the most disconnecting, disempowering habits we can adopt, yet we do it all the time. Kidding ourselves that if we relinquish responsibility, we release our conscience and put all the 'guilt' or 'shame' onto someone else.

The truth is that it does neither. It slaps shame and guilt right back at us. Casting blame passes all your personal power over to someone else, and shouts 'I am irresponsible! I'm incapable! I can't even control my own life!' Blame is paralysing, it's a disease-ridden parasite that saps all the power out of us and knocks us right into the back seat on the journey of our lives.

Sometimes the answer to a problem is to do nothing and leave it be, but only when this isn't chosen with a victim mentality. Being reactionary isn't always best; time is a great healer and sometimes space is required around a situation before it can be resolved. However, doing nothing is only an option when you know you are in a place of strong personal power, you are not being lazy or playing the victim, but choosing to do nothing as a positive, useful decision.

Of course being a victim has a few perceived short-term benefits; you relinquish not only the control over your life but also the responsibility for your life. That means that any decisions you make can be blamed on someone or something else 'I was unhappy, I'd been treated despicably, so I gave up, it wasn't my fault'.

How can you be happy, ever, if you don't take responsibility for your happiness? If you wait for life to make you happy, wait for something to come along and dig you out of the hole you are stuck in? Yes, you have been knocked down, yes you have had it tough, but you know what? If you gather the courage to look your struggles in the face and stand up to them, have the strength to fight your way out and back to happiness then you've transformed from victim to victor. You have saved yourself — and there's a whole lot more contentment and joy from that feeling than from being a responsibility-free, helpless victim.

There is absolutely nothing to be gained from allowing yourself to be a victim — of life, of someone else's actions, of your past, your future, your perceived restrictions, of anything.

As a victim, you pass your personal power firmly into someone else's hands. You give up the ability to facilitate the change you seek. You give up the ability to control your life.

Quite simply, as a victim, you give up and strap yourself into the passenger seat for the rest of your life.

Take your power back, don't play the victim to anyone or anything. Take responsibility for your life and remember that everything that happens to you is for a reason. In this game called life there is a lesson in every single thing that happens to you, tough, terrific or indifferent.

From today, right now, make the decision that you are not going to be a victim any more. You are in control, you are the pilot on this journey and you will decide what you want and how to make it happen.

I believe that everything happens for a reason; often that reason is just to show you how strong you truly can be in the face of adversity. You are exactly where you are supposed to be, right now, because of the choices you made and the path you chose to follow to this point.

Be at peace with all that has happened, all that is happening, and what will happen in the future and remember, you are never truly alone, there is always someone there for you. Those who seek shall find.

POWER UP PRACTICE

When did you last blame someone else for your mood or emotions?
....

Being honest with yourself, to what extent did you facilitate this?
....

How are you responsible for your mood?
....

What can you do to take your power back?
....

Name someone who is a hero to you...
....

What did they overcome to make you feel this way about them?
....

What of their traits do you see in yourself?
....

How can you use this side of yourself more?
....

The first step toward change is awareness. The second step is acceptance.

— Nathaniel Branden

Acceptance is Beautiful

Once the discomfort has become so acute that some sort of change needs to happen, it's time to make a decision.

You have two very simple choices: accept your life and learn to enjoy it or accept your life and choose to change it.

Before any decision, you must first learn to accept every single part of your life and yourself. This is time for the illusions to disappear. To make positive changes, you can't hide from the truth.

The Art of Acceptance is so simple and yet so complex that hundreds of books have been written about the subject. It's the very basis of the human existence — to fully accept who you are, what you are feeling and everything about you as a person in any given moment.

Before acceptance, there is a level of awareness that we need to reach. To be fully aware of ourselves and how we feel in any given moment, we need to learn to fully embrace the present. This means concentrating our focus on exactly what we have right now, who we are right now, how we feel, right now.

If I asked you right now, how do you feel, before you respond with the standard 'I'm fine', think about it. Are you happy? Are you content? Not with how you foresee your future, but right now.

How does your body feel? Are you comfortable in your bones, your muscles, and your skin? Are you comfortable? Does change feel to be bubbling up around you?

This is at the very heart of the concept of mindfulness — the practice of bringing complete focus back to the self, to calm the mind and harness full concentration on a single task or action. When you slow down time like this, you really begin to understand how you are — how you really are. Only then can you know what you need.

The curious paradox is when I accept myself just as I am, then I can change'

Carl Rogers.

Be honest with yourself. One of the worst disablers in life is our ability to kid ourselves that everything is OK and that things will change without our input.

The truth doesn't stop existing just because you're ignoring it. Peace cannot be achieved through avoidance. You have to accept it right down into your soul in order to move on from it and that means being honest, in every way. Bring your fears and weaknesses right to the front of your awareness and shine a spotlight on them. Accept who you are and where you are and what you need. Be honest.

You have to feel it to accept it, because the only way out of your fears is to go through them. The truth hurts, but it also heals.

But the beauty of acceptance runs far deeper than accepting your fears. It means accepting yourself for exactly who you are in this very moment. For every thing that you feel shame or guilt about, there are also a hundred things about you that you should be proud and grateful for.

We've just never been that great at self-promotion — it feels inappropriate, like showing off, doesn't it? But I'm not asking you to shout your abilities from the rooftops, not just yet anyway! I'm just asking you to acknowledge and accept that you're not half bad. See, it's not that hard is it?

Once you have accepted yourself, your life, your 'now' for exactly what it is, you can then decide whether you want to do something about it. Do you accept it exactly as it is and start to really enjoy it or do you accept it and start to make positive changes?

Accept yourself deep down into your soul, warts and all. Even the bits you don't like, the bits you wished you'd never done, the bits you wish you had the confidence or courage to do. Accept every decision you have made, every decision you have shirked, every thing you have ever done, not done or wanted to do.

Accept everything about your life, as it is, right now.

POWER UP PRACTICE

Today we'll practise Eating Mindfully! For your next meal, follow these simple steps...

Look at the food in front of you, notice whether you salivate and whether it makes you feel hungry. Take your time to choose one thing. Focus clearly on the movement of your hand as you lift the fork to your mouth. Feel the food touch your lips and fall into your mouth.

Imagine you have never eaten before – you are an alien on Earth and you've never seen or tried this substance before. Examine every part of the food, does it feel rough, smooth, slippery, in your mouth? Notice how you begin to chew the food, feel it moving about your mouth. Close your eyes – what can you taste? Specifically? Is it warm, cold, hot? Feel how your teeth feel on the food, take your time and chew slowly until you feel the urge to swallow. Feel the food moving down your throat.

Before you take another bite, smell the food in front of you. Observe the plate, the individual pieces of food. Carefully select a piece and smell it before putting it into your mouth. Take your time, bring your awareness back to the food, eat slowly and with observation of the process noting all the feelings you experience along the way. Repeat with the rest of the meal.

Mindful eating is an incredibly simple yet powerful practice that, if done regularly, can really change how consciously you eat and the quality of the food you eat. By bringing your full awareness to the food, you take the time to appraise it and find out if it really is what you want to eat. You'll be amazed by how much more discerning you become when you eat mindfully!

my life didn't

please me,

so

i created my life.

- Coco Chanel

Create Change

So, you've accepted yourself warts and all, and chances are that you aren't happy with everything. You've also accepted that you are responsible for where you are and where you are going and that you hold the power within you to choose the life that you WANT to live.

OK, deep breath! Now it's time for change.

Your change may be subtle, or magnificent. If it means starting again, in a relationship, or career, home or location, that's OK! Starting again doesn't mean you've failed. It means you're adapting. You're refusing to put up with the crap that you've chosen for now and you're moving on.

Don't be afraid of failure. Failure is realising that things are wrong but doing nothing about it. Failure is failing to help yourself, giving over the power of your life to your past. Failure is prematurely deciding that things will never change, for you won't allow them, and that although you know your life isn't making you happy, you are not willing to do anything about it.

When your life feels uncomfortable, this is your spirit showing you that this isn't the life for you and that there's more out there for you if you just have the courage to make the changes.

If it didn't feel uncomfortable, you wouldn't have the impetus to change. You'd likely just carry on, hoping things were going to improve. The discomfort is there to push you on, to make you change and do something about it.

The discomfort might feel like a niggle, a nagging feeling or something that just won't lie. That's your intuition alerting you as to where change will be best applied. Or, it might feel like a gaping hole, an emptiness that so far you've been filling with all the wrong things. The discomfort might feel like you just can't find your peace, everything is wrong, you are just in the wrong life, or maybe you feel you're not in it at all, just a bystander or observer, watching everyone else live while you just exist.

Whatever the discomfort, acknowledge it. Accept it and decide to do something about it. Be the change you long for. Sometimes the change isn't external – it may be that you need a new perspective on what you have, to find the beauty in what already is. However change has come knocking, so embrace it and make it work for you.

So, you don't like where you're at, or you feel a little restless right now. How do you start to create a new life for yourself?

Well, first things first. Remember — this is YOUR life. Not your parents' or your partners' or your children's or your friends' but YOUR life. What you do with YOUR life is up to YOU.

So the first thing to do is TAKE YOUR POWER BACK in order to make decisions — don't go running to the nearest person to ask them what you should do, take your power back and decide to plan your future yourself.

If it's not making you happy then it is up to you to change it — to create the life you want. Don't expect anyone else to do it for you. Those closest to you will want to put their suggestions in, for they will think they know what you want. And depending how bossy they can be (calling all mothers!) they will either be encouraging or rather persuading. But how can they truly know what you want? Only you know what is right for you and how your life needs to be to make you happy. One step at a time, then.

Check out the 'wheel of opportunity' on the next page – this is the start of the creation of your limitless, happy life.

Look at each section: health, soul, love, home, friendship, career, money and family. Which areas need to change? What is it about each one that doesn't feel right? What would you like to have in those areas? What is missing from your life?

Sketch your own wheel and write into each section what you WANT. It can be as simple as 'TO FEEL LOVED', 'MORE MONEY', "TO MOVE HOUSE' or 'TO FEEL MORE CONNECTED' or as detailed as '4 bed house' or 'to be a freelance graphic artist'. Don't limit your imagination and your potential. If you run out of space, make yourself another wheel on the next page and add some more! You have a lifetime to go out and achieve this so BE BOLD and GO FOR IT!

As you start to fill out the wheel, try not to allow self-sabotage to get in the way. There is no point doing this exercise if you're going to put yourself down and muck up your plans before you even get going.

the wheel of opportunity

The idea of this exercise isn't to rush into putting these dreams into action, it's about taking control over your thoughts, feelings and emotions, taking your power back and making sure that your next move is YOUR next move.

Over the next few days, work on your wheel of fortune and enjoy it. Don't think about 'how', just work out 'what'. Make it colourful and interesting, making it appealing, show yourself what you want and show the Universe what you want.

Now simply by writing it down, you have put it out there, you have started to make it happen, without even doing a thing. You have ignited your intention and started to clear the way in your cluttered mind for inspiration and action.

Dream big, allow yourself to really enjoy the projection of your possible new future.

"I was working in Telesales and absolutely hated every minute of it. But I had very few qualifications when I left school so felt I'd little choice when it came to getting a job.

What I really wanted to do was be a firefighter, but that just seemed to be really competitive and out of reach.

After some encouragement from my sister, I reluctantly decided to speak to a mentor at a local college and found out that I didn't need any formal qualifications to be a firefighter, but that I needed to demonstrate some fairly general skills like effective communication skills; integrity, composure and a reassuring manner and the ability to follow instructions, amongst others.

So I rejigged my CV and bit the bullet — I wrote off to my six local fire stations to see if they had any openings. One not far from my house wrote a letter back saying that I was welcome to go for a day to see what they did and then potentially work on a voluntary basis at weekends so they could assess my abilities for when a suitable job came up. There was a waiting list but I figured that I had nothing better to do than wait, so I went for it.

I've been volunteering for two months now and everyone seems really happy with me. I've had to improve my physical fitness to but this has been great because I've met some new friends working out at the gym attached to the station after work, so I also feel far better about myself. There's a full time firefighter job coming up next month and when I've completed a course in the next two weeks, I know I have a very good chance of getting it."

Steve, 22, Perth, Australia

Stop holding on to intimate relationships that make you unhappy. Start looking out for yourself when it comes to intimate relationships. It's better to WAIT, and give your hand to someone who will never let go, rather than holding on to the outside of a hand that has never fully opened for you.

If someone wants you in their life, they'll make room for you. You shouldn't have to fight for a spot. Never, ever insist on yourself to someone who continuously overlooks your worth. Remember, anyone can come into your life and say how much they love you. But it takes someone really special to stay in your life and show you how much they love you. So slow it down. True love is worth the wait.

You will only ever live the life you create for yourself

Lucy Day, The Modern Medium

Your life is yours alone. Others can try to persuade you, but they can't decide for you. They can walk with you, but not in your shoes. So make sure the path you decide to walk aligns with your own intuition and desires, and don't be scared to switch paths or pave a new one when it makes sense.

Remember, it's always better to be at the bottom of the ladder you want to climb than at the top of the one you don't. Be productive and patient. And realise that patience is not about waiting, but the ability to keep a positive attitude while working hard for what you believe in. This is your life, and it is made up entirely of your choices. May your actions speak louder than your words. May your life preach louder than your lips. May your success be your noise in the end.

And if life only teaches you one thing, let it be that taking a passionate leap is always worth it. Even if you have no idea where you're going to land, be brave enough to step up to the edge of the unknown, and listen to your heart.

POWER UP PRACTICE

In the next few days, start to write down what you need to achieve your desires in each area of your 'Wheel of Opportunity'. These needs should be specific to be of any use for your future planning.

For example, if you are working on moving house, then you could specify how much money you need to have the type and size house you would like. How much will your mortgage be? Or will you rent? If so, how much money do you need for a deposit and for each month's payment? In what areas will you look? Whereabouts do you want to live, and so on.

Work on each segment in turn until you have a practical illustration of how you would like each area of your life to be.

Area of Opportunity	*Desire*	*Specific Details*
e.g. Career	A new challenge. More Money.	Change of career, align with interests. Possibly own business. Study to add skills.

Sit on this list for a few days, rather than rush off to try and solve everything at once. Let your mind and your spirit start to work on solutions. Allow life to start working on your vision of your future, segment by segment.

Come back to the pages and choose one area only to start working on. This segment will naturally kick start changes in other areas and will allow you to concentrate your efforts rather than trying to scatter your energies everywhere.

This way, you are starting to formulate a plan.

Happiness is subjective, what makes you happy will be very different to what makes someone else smile, so allow yourself to dream, to plan, to play. Don't limit yourself, write down exactly what you would like and enjoy the process.

As you work through each area, you'll end up with an illustration of your potential future and can then take your time figuring out how to make it happen. Think of it as something to look forward to, something to strive for and to change and adapt as you go along. Plus, you'll feel like you're putting plans into action, which is incredibly empowering. Every time you think of something else, add it to your plan. Allow it to change, expand or reduce. Nothing is set in stone.

A basic plan and a small step forward is all you need to move into the future you desire.

you have **peace,** the old woman said, when you make it with yourself.

- Mitch Albom

Forgive yourself

- TO ERR IS HUMAN -

Make a pact with yourself today to not be defined by the choices you made in your past.

As humans, we have free will — the ability to navigate our own lives making our own choices and decisions and as a result, learning to live with these decisions. Decision-making starts at a very young age and doesn't really stop until we exit this world.

Some of our decisions may not have worked out as we expected. Some were made with purely unselfish motivation; others were made with only us in mind and therefore impacted negatively on others. Some of our decisions hurt us; some hurt other people or souls.

We often make decisions knowing that they are not the best choices. Our gut instinct often tries to tell us that they are wrong, but we ignore it, because we retain a hope that it 'might work out'. Decisions come with the risk that they might go wrong. They come with the guilt that they might not have been right for others, the impact of the responsibility that our decisions come with.

Own your decisions, own your choices, whether they had a negative or positive impact on your life or that of others. When you are honest about things that you might, in hindsight, not be proud of, you remove the risk of adding insult to injury by denying or lying about them. Take responsibility for your actions and own your mistakes, but don't let them define you.

At the end of the day, if you're not making decisions, you're not living, you're not learning. If you don't take responsibility for the choices in your life, then you are a passenger, and a passenger learns nothing but observation. You have to be involved, to be the pilot, to be in charge, in order to grow.

Sometimes the greatest thing to come out of all your decision-making isn't what you get for it, but what you learn from it. A happy, successful life, after all, is not a life empty of problems, but one that has illustrated your ability to rise above them.

The only mistake is not learning from the decisions you make. If something you have chosen to do turns out badly in your eyes, then try not to do the very same thing again! It's that simple. Learn.

What worked in one situation may not work in the next, and vice versa. So remember that just because you tried and it didn't work, doesn't mean it won't work this time with effort and maybe a change in perspective and attitude.

Perfection is an illusion

Lucy Day, The Modern Medium

Perfectionism is a funny thing. Few of us seek it in others but regularly apply it to our own lives — chastising ourselves if we feel we haven't made the grade. Whether it comes from always trying to live up to our parents' unrealistic expectations, or is a manifestation of our own lack of self-esteem, we all have an element of expected perfection in our lives.

We are so quick to judge ourselves, to put ourselves down, to decide that we are failures, far quicker than we would be with a friend or partner. When we speak to them, we are full of love and encouragement and would likely motivate them to 'keep going' because 'you've got this'. Imagine how much happier you would be if you spoke to yourself like this? If you told yourself that the choices you made in the past don't matter, that you deserve to be happy and you're going to keep going until you are, that you know deep down inside you, you have the ability to choose well for yourself and along the way you're going to see how strong and capable you are.

It's often in the hardest moments that you realise your true strength, what you are capable of. When times are tough and the difficulty is due to a decision you made in your past, well that's when the guilt and self-blame come in. But that doesn't help you, it just drags you down. Think of a friend who has made decisions in the past that have led to their unhappiness. Would you tell them that they have failed and they have messed up so they just have to sit and dwell in their unhappiness and accept this is life and it won't change? Or would you tell them that they got themselves into it but they can get themselves out of it? Would you tell them that they are stronger than they realise and that they can take their power back and learn from their mistakes and never make them again? Of course you would. Now, be a friend to yourself and take some of your own medicine.

"For years I felt trapped in an abusive relationship. I knew it was wrong and that neither of us were making the other happy but I just couldn't see a way out. In the end, it took for me to have a complete nervous breakdown before I realized that I couldn't go on like this. It wasn't that he was violent, he never laid a finger on me, but the emotional abuse was just as bad. Four years after we finally separated, because he had found someone else, I was still attracting the same kind of guy, controlling, aggressive and manipulative. I'd gone from one awful relationship to another.

I met a woman on a train on the way home from work one evening and we got chatting. She told me that she had lost her husband to cancer three years previously but that she had just met a new man and was going to meet him. The way she described her husband and their relationship really opened my eyes. The respect and love that they had had for each other was beautiful. More than that though, the new chap she described sounded amazing too.

At first, I felt quite jealous; why couldn't I meet men like that? Why do I get into such negative relationships? Then I realised — it was my choice. I was doing this to myself. I hadn't learned the first time and had just allowed habit to take over my life — going along with what I knew, even though it wasn't good for me, or what I really wanted.

That chance meeting changed my life. I made a deal with myself to choose love, to value myself and only to allow a man in my life that valued and loved me too. Properly. That was two years ago and I am now engaged to a wonderful, calm and peaceful man, someone who loves me for me, someone who I know is always there for me. Life is awesome."

Janet, 36, Redfern, UK

If you're too afraid of failure, you will be too afraid to move. You need to keep making decisions, to keep moving forward. When you allow the feeling of failure to paralyse you you'll go nowhere, you'll stagnate.

Do you know the difference between a master and an amateur? The master has failed more times than the amateur has even tried. Behind every amazing creation is a hundred failed attempts to make it but we only ever see the final result — we don't see the toil and strife behind getting to the finishing line.

The fact is that sometimes, things have to go really wrong before they start going right. Nobody makes the right decision first time; we all have to feel our way through this life. Success is getting up, dusting yourself off and getting back on the right path. Failure is sitting down and refusing to move for fear of making the wrong decision.

Forgive yourself; do not be defined by the choices you have made. We are all just humans, no matter how important or insignificant we feel we are. Life throws lemons at us all the time and knowing how to turn them into lemonade — that only comes with experience and learning — from making it too sour and knowing to add more sugar... the trick is to try to enjoy the process.

POWER UP PRACTICE

Scanning through your recent past, reflect on two areas that didn't work out favourably for you. Take your time to think about how these experiences affected you.

What have you learned from these experiences?

....

What changes could you make if faced with a similar situation in the future?

....

Look for the lessons in these experiences – how have they helped you to grow?

....

➔ **Remember to empower yourself by being grateful for these experiences, for getting through them and seeing the positive that they have served you.**

the greatest gifts you can give your children are the roots of responsibility and the wings of independence.

- Denis Waitley

9

Take Responsibility

- IT'S YOUR LIFE -

Who is responsible for your happiness?

Do you take 100% responsibly for your thoughts and feelings on a daily basis or do you pass the blame and therefore power to someone else?

Some people believe they can really only be happy when in a relationship. Others are happy only when their partner is happy. Some blame the lack of a partner for their unhappiness yet others blame their partner for their unhappiness.

When things go wrong in a relationship, or cracks begin to show, so often we start to focus on the changes we wish to see in our partner, to make us happy. We can get so focused on wanting them to change that we feel powerless and overwhelmed when they don't – pushing our personal power firmly into their hands.

Since when did getting into a relationship mean handing the power over your happiness to your partner? Who was responsible for your happiness before you met? You or your previous partner?

As a child, we hope to be looked after so well by our parents that they contribute to our happiness by making life fun, exciting and interesting, filling our days with things to do, showering us with love and laughter. Goodness knows that as kids we could be demanding — like a very needy audience wanting the show to go on all day every day. But as soon as we come of age, rather than taking that baton and realising it's now our job to make ourselves happy, many of us transfer this responsibility from our parents to our partners.

Happy in love but unhappy out of love. How many people do you know who go from relationship to relationship, unable to be happy and alone? It's almost an epidemic now, the need to be in a partnership. Not the desire but the need.

Love is the greatest power stealer ever. It's as if we fall in love and immediately allow our power to go straight into the arms of our partner. 'Go ahead, take it all — have me!'

What made you fall in love in the first place? Did your partner fall for you because you allowed them and their actions to dictate how you felt and acted? No. Your partner fell in love with you, the independent you, not the needy you.

If you allow your happiness to lie solely in the power of your partner then you are relinquishing all control. If they have a crappy day, you have a crappy day. If they are away, you miss them and feel sad. If you don't have a partner at all, then you are unhappy until you have one.

Time to take your power back into your control and control your own happiness. Remember that it is not your partner's responsibility to make you happy and having a partner won't instantly make you happy either. Putting such expectations on another person is not only unfair pressure but also puts the power firmly in their hands, whether they are aware of it or not.

"There is only one success — to be able to live life in your own way"

Christopher Morley

As long as you're not hurting anyone else, live your life YOUR way. Sometimes we get lost in trying to live for someone else, trying to meet their expectations and doing things just to impress them. Seeking acceptance and approval is a huge power stealer. So many of us, even by middle age, continue to seek approval from our parents, friends or partners, before we feel fully accepting of our actions and decisions.

The thing with taking responsibility for your own life, your own happiness, is that when things don't go as planned, aren't as smooth as you'd hoped, or you make what you later feel was a mistake, then you and only you can take responsibility for those things. There is a great blessing in owning your own life.

When you take responsibility for your life — great, tough or just plain ugly, you accept that you have made your own choices, you are not placing blame at anyone else's door — you are 100% responsible for the outcome of your decisions and actions.

Responsibility is for the brave. To take the power back over your life you have to be brave. But fortune favours the brave and when you are making choices based on what makes you happy, you are 100% responsible for all the happy outcomes too. You did it!

Live for yourself, not for others' preconceptions of who you should be. Not because someone told you that you should, or they think it's right. Trust your intuition. Remember that the one person who knows you the best is you. You are the guru of you!

POWER UP PRACTICE

How much power does your partner have over your happiness?

....

When did you last do something just for you?

....

Is the career you are in one that you chose for yourself? Or did someone else choose it for you?

....

When you were a child, what did you want to be when you grew up?

....

What changed?

....

What hobbies do you have?

....

What makes your heart beat a little faster?

....

If you could do one thing every day of your life, what would it be?

....

peace comes from within.

do not seek it without.

- Gautama Buddha

Look inside for Answers

- TRUST YOURSELF -

As children, our parents and peers teach us literally everything we know. But at a point the weaning begins and they start to back off, allowing us to start making our own decisions, loosening the ties that bind us to them and encouraging maturity.

Some of us only start to gain control of our personal power as teenagers, finally making decisions about our own life either independently or with advice and help from our parents.

As adults, we are truly free to make our own choices but so many of us are afraid of making a mistake that we don't trust our own minds. We ask the opinions of those we trust and take their advice before really considering our own. Without our personal power, we effectively put our lives in the hands of someone or something else.

"I keep asking people for advice, but no one really seems to know what I can do. Everyone keeps telling me that I need an identity and should look at getting a job. I know that's true but I don't know what to do! It would be so much easier if someone would just offer me something. Being a single Mum of an 18 month old, I have no idea what I would be good at; it's been so long since I worked."

Louise, 24

When did you last sit and really think, spending quality time considering a problem? With the web making answers about everything so accessible now, it is likely that you have searched online for an answer to your problems before, or instead of, turning inward and thinking for yourself.

The truth is that whilst your parents have always wanted the best for you, they may have had their own preconceived ideas about success, what they thought you could do, what they wanted you to do. Their advice is not without prejudice; far from it.

Your friends are exactly the same as your parents, in that their advice comes with a huge helping of opinion plus their own hidden agendas, and could end up pointing you in completely the wrong direction, even if it is well meant.

Asking someone with knowledge of the area you are contemplating can of course help. It's always good to have a chat with those in the know and get a rounded view of things. But those who listen with an open mind learn the most —someone may tell you that they think you should 'do this or that', but you still need to step back and ask yourself 'is this what I want?'

Only you know your own mind. Only you have the power over your choices.

When it comes to making decisions in your life, the power needs to be firmly in your hands. If you constantly give the power over important decisions to someone else, then you will be living their life, not your own. And who are you going to blame when it all goes wrong?

When it comes to making decisions for ourselves, we have a secret weapon — our intuition, that little voice that whispers in your head and makes you know in your gut when something is right or very wrong. When you stop doing what everybody else wants you to do and start following your own intuition, you will find exactly what you are looking for.

Trust yourself.

If something doesn't feel right, stop. Listen to your feelings. If you can't make a decision about what to do there and then, put some space around it. Give it time. Allow the answer to come to you naturally. There's far more value in allowing your subconscious to quietly work away in the background, seeking an answer that is true to you, than in making reactionary decisions which create more problems down the line.

Listen to those feelings. Try to distinguish between the fear of the unknown and your intuition. Fear feels out of control, emotional, scary — intuition feels off, wrong, unemotional, irritating, persuasive. You will soon learn to feel the difference between the two.

The more you listen to your intuition, the more you will eliminate those 'I knew I shouldn't have done that!' situations, because you will start to act, respond and change in the moment, rather than afterwards.

Only you know what you want. Only you know what is best for you. The answers have always been within, from the day you were born. They just need you to turn up the volume on that quiet voice which whispers YOUR truths. You have all the power and knowledge and insight into your journey that you will ever need.

Trust your intuition and you will take off with ease.

POWER UP PRACTICE

You don't have to access a meditative state to tune into your intuition – you just need to train yourself to 'hear' it. By creating a way of interpreting 'yes and no' intuitively you can learn to distinguish between your intuition, fear and hope.

Step One: Learn how 'Yes' feels.

Practise thinking of something that you know is a positive fact. For example, it may be that you 'love your pet dog', or you are 'happy about going on holiday'. When you ask yourself whether this is true, how does the 'yes' sensation feel? Where in your body do you feel this positive sensation? Many people feel their intuition just above their belly button – that's why we call it 'gut instinct'. Others feel it in their whole body, or just their stomach area. Keep practicing how 'yes' feels. Intuition usually comes with a lack of emotion and it tends to feel true, coming with conviction, so learn to feel this within your body.

Step Two: Learn to feel 'No'

Practise thinking of something you don't align yourself with, perhaps something from your past that you don't wish to ever repeat, or something you have recently decided not to do. Think about or imagine that situation happening. Feel how 'no' creates a negative sensation in your body. You may even draw a breath or shake your head. Remember this is not about fear — fear is emotional and comes with descriptions, images and illusions. Intuition is factual, blunt and clear. Learn to distinguish between the two by practicing the feelings. This takes time so try to enjoy finding out how your intuition feels to you.

Step Three: Trust your Feelings

Choose a situation that you are not sure about. Simply ask yourself – should I do X? Notice the changes in your body – feel your intuition instantly respond. It may even feel like a little electric shock in your skin. Learn your triggers. Your intuition will answer faster than your mind can create a thought. Push subsequent thoughts out of the way and remember this is about feeling. You may find this easier to do in a quiet space, somewhere that you can have some peace, rather than rush to a conclusion.

Remember, this isn't just about learning to feel your intuition, but also about learning to trust yourself. It will take time, so don't expect instant results. It's a process that you can practise when you wish and will find that over time you become more and more aware of the answers being inside you.

➔**Learning to use your intuition is all about learning to feel your own answers deep inside, connecting with your soul. Your soul talks very loudly once you allow yourself to truly hear it. Listen…**

there are
some things
i can't control
and that's just the
way it is.

- Susanne Colasanti

Choose your fights Wisely

Mental strength is like muscle strength — no one has an unlimited supply. So why waste your energy and power worrying and moaning about things you can't change?

For some people, it's the weather. For others, it's politics, family disputes or even the decline in television programming quality. Whatever it is, complaining takes up an awful lot of energy when there's very little you can do to change it.

So rather than allow these negative energies to take up your valuable time, determine if this fight is worth even a moment of your input. Is it your issue to take up? Are you being dragged in, or do you want to be involved? Can you do anything positive for the cause?

If you're directly involved and you can do something positive to improve the situation, then by all means head on in and weave your magic, otherwise let things be.

When it comes to family problems, the people involved can really only help themselves, so listen, help when you are asked, but otherwise just let the situation work itself out. You are not your family; you are just a family member, so distance your energy a little from where you know you are not involved. Family gossip is one of the most harmful energies you can join in, and it can split a family in two. If it's not your problem, don't make it so.

When it comes to politics, make a sensible and learned vote and withdraw your energy. Unless you're going to directly do something about changing who is in power, or what they are doing or how they are doing it, moaning about it will not make it change.

Alongside the government, other systems, such as work, also offer a constant arena for battles that we can't win. We join a company which has been doing things a certain way under a specific directorship for years. When we start, we don't notice things that annoy us but over time we become aware of areas that are uncomfortable or unappetising. These problems then become the focus of our attention. But again, unless you are in a position of power, are willing to make an effort to positively change the company and its ways, what is the point of moaning about it?

We are all guilty of moaning about our partners and wishing that they too would change. But truly, who are we to change them? How would we feel if we heard our partner telling someone that they just 'wish he/she would change'? We would be defensive, 'this is me! Take me as I am!' Indeed, no matter how negative our partner's ways seem to us, we are not in a position to change them. Things that were once attractive to us can become a turn off, or annoying later down the line. But note that it is often us who has changed our tastes and tolerance, not our partner who has suddenly become irritating.

There are so many difficulties in our lives that it truly makes no sense to go looking for trouble.

The only person you can change is YOU. The only power you have is over YOURSELF. The only power worth focusing on is YOUR OWN. Make yourself the agent of change in your life and leave all the other battles to those who have the power to make a change.

You'll be amazed by how much better you feel when you choose to release concerns over things you can't control, in much the same way that it amazes you how quickly things escalate negatively when you get involved in things that you shouldn't.

Releasing anything that you can't control brings lightness into your life, clarity, calm and peace of mind. When you relinquish your concern for that which doesn't serve you, the relief is palpable and overwhelmingly powerful.

You release time and energy that can be used positively in your own areas of influence. You become carefree, get a skip in your step and emanate a harmonious energy that attracts contentment and happiness to you.

Pure Bliss.

POWER UP PRACTICE

Imagine you lived in a perfect world. What would it look like? How would it feel to live there? What would you experience that you don't right now? What major differences would you see?

Draw a little picture of it in your mind or on paper.

Take a mental step back from this world. Ask yourself... how can YOU be the change that our world needs, to come in line with this perfect version?

➔ **Remember, you have the power to be the changes you wish to see.**

The cure
for most obstacles is,
be decisive.

- George Weinberg

Become Decisive

One of the greatest ways to sap your personal power is by doing nothing at all.

Don't confuse planning to do something with doing it. Happiness never comes to look for you while you wait around thinking about it.

You are what you do, not what you say you'll do. You are the product of your decisions, your understanding, growth and development from the lessons life has given you. That means making decisions, accepting change and moving forward.

Of course we delay making decisions, often through the fear of failure or making a mistake and getting it wrong. But knowledge is useless without action. It's possible now to research just about everything conceivable on the internet, so we can all recite information on a subject, but it's only by doing something, having that experience, that we can enjoy life.

So, by now you know that you want change, you know that you need change, so it's time to make that change. Time to make those decisions and be responsible for the outcome. Planning is all well and good but the truth is that great things don't come to those who wait; they come to those who work on moving forward with patience for the outcome.

Ask yourself what's really important and then have the courage to build your life around your answer. Remember, if you wait until you feel 100% ready to begin, you'll likely be waiting the rest of your life.

Impulsive decisions are almost always better than no decisions at all. Indecisiveness just delays while poor decisions teach us to make better ones. In the end, we most often regret the chances we didn't take, the relationships we were afraid to have, and the decisions we waited too long to make.

There is a very easy way to know whether your decision is right or not, in fact it is so simple you will want it to be more complex!

Choose out of love, not fear.

Lucy Day, *The Modern Medium*

When you make decisions based on fears, you choose wrong. Every time. Fear is, after all, an illusion — it's the product of taking your past negative experiences, mixing them with your imagination and projecting them into your future. Fears are not real. But love? Love *is* real. Tangible, real, based on your own experiences, it touches your heart and soul and makes you truly happy, safe, content and calm. Love heals everything.

Think of love as positive and fear as negative — light and dark, like and dislike. Judge every decision on these attributes and make sure that the very next time you go to make a fundamental decision about your future, you ask yourself this — am I choosing this out of love, because I want it, because it makes me feel happy and content and I like it? Or am I making this decision because of fear — the fear of missing out, of failure, of doing the wrong thing, of upsetting someone, of getting it wrong?

When you choose out of love, positivity, happiness, you choose right every time. Guaranteed.

So take action and make positive changes. Action and change are often resisted just at the point that you most need them – the tipping point. So be bold, get a hold of yourself, take your power back and have discipline. Discipline is choosing what you really want for your future over what is ok for now. It's the difference between hiding in your comfort zone and throwing yourself out into the unknown. If it's not really all that comfortable in that little habitual place you've been hiding in, then you know the answer already.

"I graduated from university with a first class honours degree in computing science and got a much sought after graduate post with a big telecommunications company. I worked there for 5 years, initially I thought it was great - I enjoyed the intellectual buzz, there was a good social side, I was good at the work. But after a couple of years I realised that the harder I worked and the more I gave, the more the company wanted and expected - more work, tighter schedules, and I started to question what I was doing it all for. I realised this wasn't what I wanted out of life, I wanted to be able to make a difference to people. I decided I wanted to become a paramedic, but also realised I was going to have to take a big pay cut to make a change.

I had a mortgage, so I set in place a 2 year plan, saved huge chunks of my pay each month and when I felt I had enough saved up, I started to look at applying to the ambulance service. Unfortunately, (or fortunately, with hindsight) there was a recruitment freeze at the time. A couple of months later I happened to pick up the local paper and spotted an advert for a critical care and anaesthetic technician. I contacted them, applied, and got the job. They couldn't believe I accepted, as it was more than a 50% pay cut for me!

When I started it was like landing on Mars, I had gone from being an expert in my previous job to the person who knew nothing. But fast forward 6 months and everything had clicked into place. The person assigned to be my mentor became my best friend for life and I loved the work and patients. I quickly moved up through pay bands and got promoted to senior staff. At this stage I decided to move house and got a little end terrace, very different from the kind of place I would have got if I still worked for my previous company.

After being there 6 months, there was a knock on the door one Saturday night and a tall dark handsome stranger introduced himself as my neighbour from 4 doors down. He wanted to know if I knew anything about builders in the next field wanting to put a road through the hedge and he had a map. He said his map might look strange, as it was a hillwalking map. I said I liked hillwalking too and invited him in for a drink. 11 years later here we are with our 2 beautiful children."

Fiona, 38, Northern Ireland

Procrastination makes easy things hard, hard things harder.

Mason Cooley

Putting something off makes it instantly harder and scarier; you're widening the gap between possible and impossible. What we don't start today won't be finished by tomorrow and there's nothing more stressful than the lingering of an unfinished task.

So, go on, just do it.

POWER UP PRACTICE

Write this affirmation on ten sticky notes. Stick one to each mirror in your house, at eye height. Stick one to the door of the fridge and one to the back of the front door, one on your bedside table, to your diary and your laptop – basically anywhere or anything you look at regularly. For two days, every time you see this affirmation, say it out loud or in your head.

➜ **Burn these words metaphorically into your mind – they give you the power to change your life!**

The minute you settle for less than you deserve, you get even less than you settled for.

— Maureen Dowd

Aim High

- DON'T SETTLE -

How much you value yourself dictates how much you feel you deserve. Often this is far less than reality. It's amazing, isn't it, how when a friend is being mistreated by a partner, we can clearly see the issues. We are quick to tell the friend that they deserve more, that the partner is terrible and that they would be better without than to accept this grief. But when we look at our own relationship issues, we find it far harder to see our own true value, we often expect and accept far less for our own lives.

This can be said for just about every aspect of life that touches us — from our careers, relationships, family relationships, home, health, money. We really do limit ourselves and accept far less than we would if we could look at our life from an outer perspective.

We start off with great ambitions, with ideas about big houses, amazing jobs, travelling the world and marrying our soul mates, but the gradual chipping away of self esteem caused by the outcome of our early decisions can mean that by the time we are only in our early 20's, we have already started to limit our expectations.

One of the main areas in which many of us settle for less than we should is within our personal relationships. We may start off with expectations of what we will accept, but as soon as we start to compromise, often for an easy life at the time, and overlook poor behaviour and bad habits, we find ourselves settling for far less than what we should.

For those of us who haven't found 'the one' by a certain age, the pressure of being settled down, married and starting a family can be so strong that we settle for the next person who comes along, no matter how unsuited or inappropriate the relationship. But, just like poorly skimmed walls, before long the cracks start to show and no amount of papering over can cover up the problems with the relationship.

Far better to remain on your own, with your personal power intact and your heart in one piece than to accept a second best relationship for fear of not getting anything else. Far better to wait for 'the one' than accept 'anyone' just to have company. Marrying for companionship just doesn't work unless you're retired, both have the same goal and motivations and like going on cruises!

I see many people who have settled for second best in an early relationship, had children and then gone through very messy divorces, child custody cases and financial crises, only to find 'the one' some years later, finally relieved that they were out there.

It's not just relationships where we settle for second best, so many of us have settled for mediocre jobs because 'it's money' or 'what else can I do?' and are left unhappy, unmotivated, discontented and trapped by circumstance.

Aim high, don't let 'half baked' be your mantra. With a challenge comes a feeling of achievement, of success. Step out of your comfort zone — what's the worst that can happen? Better to be alone and available for Mr/Mrs.

Right to come along than to be trapped in an unhappy relationship. Better to be looking for a more appropriate job or studying for greater skills than be stuck in a job that makes you hate getting out of bed in the morning.

If you've settled for second best and you know it, then you also know that first is out there — so go find it, be brave.

My ability to conquer my fears is limitless; my potential to succeed is infinite

Plain and simple, you have no limits but those you place on yourself. What kind of life do you want? What is stopping you? What barriers are you imposing on yourself? This affirmation will help you address all of the boundaries.

POWER UP PRACTICE

To aim high in life, you need to know what you want. To find out what you want, you need to know what you value. Chances are you know your basic values, but haven't spent time really analysing what is truly important to you.

A power up exercise in value mapping will help you understand a little more about what makes you tick and what to aim for in experiences, choices, relationships and anything you agree to engage in.

Step 1: Ask yourself "What's important to me in life?"
Write down anything and everything — whatever pops into your mind!

Step 2: Review each statement you have written
Anything you have put down that you can 'do' or 'have' is probably not a value. Ask yourself "What does that give me?" until you get to a value. For example, 'having money' as a value could be 'security' or 'being happy' as a value could be 'companionship' or 'trust' or 'recognition' – delve into the desire until it forms a value.

Step 3: Narrow down the list to a top 10.
Put the most important at the top.
For example...
1) Honesty
2) Trust
3) Companionship
4) Security
5) Loyalty

You now have a list of personal values. Feel free to edit the list as much as you need until it feels completely right - intuitively right (remember to use your 'yes/no' sensations).

We'll use this list later so keep it safe!

people are always **blaming** their circumstances for what they are. i don't believe in circumstances. the people who get on in this world are the people who get up and look for the circumstances they want, and, if they can't find them, make them.

— George Bernard Shaw

Stop Complaining

- START LIVING -

Stop worrying and complaining! Nothing sucks the life out of you more than the constant outpouring of your own misery.

Switch that mindset and pull your power back. Start focusing on the things you can control and do something about them. Those who complain the most accomplish the least and when you spend time worrying, you're simply using your imagination to create things you don't want. It's usually only as positive or challenging as you think it is going to be.

Your choice of words has an incredible power over you — they can be so disabling if you let them. Think of your mind as a very powerful computer with an acute autocorrect and a predictive text option. When you go to say something, your mind will select the words that you use most often, your unique dialogue. If you fill your dialogue with negative, uneasy, unhappy words, you will find that even if you don't mean to, you will continue to speak in a negative and unhappy way. Your computer is programmed to follow the path of least resistance. In many ways this is why people find depression so hard to get out of, because the chemical pathways that release the hormones related to negative thinking are used the most often. The brain is programmed to feel sad, to find fault, to be down and depressed.

Fill your garden with flowers, before it fills with weeds

Lucy Day, The Modern Medium

Learn to use positive language, take control of your mind and your reactions. Take the power back from the habitual side of your brain and stop it from moaning. Stop it from seeing the negative in a situation, from disabling you by instilling fear into you. Open your mind and heart to the potential that life has to offer, not the misery.

Complaining is a complete waste of energy, so put your energy into making the situation better. If you don't like it and it's within your control — fix it!

Don't talk about it, just do it. Don't whine about it, resolve it.

You cannot have a positive life and a negative mind.

Joyce Meyer

We've all spent hours, sometimes on a daily basis, wrestling with events in our minds that aren't even likely to happen, worrying about things to the point where we come full circle and get absolutely nowhere.

Negativity breeds negativity in the same way that positivity breeds positivity. We get what we give off. See yourself as a magnet; you either send out negative energy and repel everything around you or you harness positivity and happiness and you get the very same back. It's natural, when feeling down, to look for evidence of others' misfortune, to, in a way, help us to feel less alone in our worries. But this helps no one, it just reinforces the feeling of lack, desperation and helplessness. Be mindful of the 'pity party' and remember that misery enjoys company!

The problem with negative thinking is that it carries us away like a riptide — we can end up so far from shore that we are pulled right under by the strength of the waves of negativity. But you have a choice — you can accept and embrace negativity and live a life of fear and worry, or you can choose love, happiness and positivity. It might feel like you're kidding yourself at first, putting a brave face on, but soon that fakery will turn into reality. You have to fake it to make it.

Even if our unhappiness is the cause of someone else's actions, no matter how hard your journey seems, you have the choice of two paths — the light path of positivity or the heavy path of misery. Remember, there is always an answer to every difficult situation. It only seems impossible to find a way out until you succeed. No matter which path you travel on you will end up at the same destination; the only question is whether you complain all the way there or arrive with a smile on your face!

POWER UP PRACTICE

Grab a piece of paper and draw a line down on the middle, title the left hand side 'Limiting Belief' and the right hand side 'Power Statement'.

Throughout the day, check your mind for any negative thoughts or beliefs that get in the way of the happy, limitless future you are creating. Write them down on the left hand side of the paper.

At the end of the day, in the right hand column write a statement that counteracts the thought you had, using all of the liberating knowledge you now have about taking back your power. For example:

Limiting Belief	Power Statement
I am useless in love.	*My ability to love and be loved flows with ease.*
I can't do this job any more.	*I am in control of my career.*
	If I'm not happy, I will change it.

Power up your life and shoot down those limiting beliefs.

→ **You have the power to create your happiness.**

have no fear
of perfection
– you'll never reach
it.

– Salvador Dalí

Drop the concept of Perfection

Many of us spend our formative years caught up in competition, being judged out of 10 or 100 on essays, homework and projects, being marked from A— E on our abilities. For some, achieving top marks is key to our happiness, and for others, being average is a comfortable point. But those who do brilliantly and those who come bottom of the class often share the same fears — of not being perfect.

The truth is that there is no such thing as perfect success in the same way that we never fail perfectly either. Seeking extremes is completely pointless. We all fail, for without failure we would never learn. We must experience the dark to recognise the light. We must fail in order to learn what it is to keep going against the odds. Perfection neither exists, nor is attainable.

Life is a series of imperfect moments interspersed with hope and possibilities, which are truly endless.

We put such expectations on ourselves its no wonder that we experience 'failure' on a daily basis. Take common diets, lifestyles, and health regimes — there are so many that set unrealistic goals from day one. When you did you last try to 'cut out alcohol for a month' or 'go vegan overnight'? To expect our minds and bodies to take on extreme changes is just unrealistic. We inevitably end up falling off the wagon and then feeling even more crap about ourselves because we perceived our failure.

When we expect perfection, we give power to perfection and if we don't achieve it, we feel powerless, useless, just plain rubbish. But we've set ourselves up to fail! How unfair we are to ourselves. We learn far quicker not to accept the same level of perfection from others, but take a lot longer to accept a lesser, more appropriate level of achievement in ourselves.

Life is not about the destination, but the journey, and that journey will always be littered with potholes, one-way systems, dead ends and T-junctions. We need to learn through our choices, our decisions, and no one can claim to have always made the right one, done the right thing, had the right result. All we can do is try.

There's an old joke: 'how do you eat an elephant? One bite at a time!' and I love how appropriate it is to this scenario. Life is that elephant, we can't just swallow it down whole. We need to take it piece by piece, accept that it's a process, not a race. When we expect perfectionism from ourselves in all aspects of our life, we just set ourselves up to fail. All we can do is take one step forward and keep moving, never stopping, never looking back.

The trick to retaining your personal power along the journey is to make sure that experiencing failure never takes your power away from you. If you allow failure to stop you, to knock your confidence to the point that you become static, then failure has stolen your power.

Get back up, dust yourself off, gather up your Personal Power, put your game face on and get back out there.

You're not aiming for perfection, you're aiming for experiences and opportunities, to head in the right direction and learn what you can on the way.

If those around you have extreme or inappropriate expectations of you, if you feel you have to keep up to be accepted, then the fact is that they are not worth trying to impress. Real love is unconditional, not based on what you achieve or what you do. If a friend doesn't like you for who you are deep down, then they are not a true friend. If your partner has unrealistic expectations of you, then they do not value the real you and are not worth your love.

If you believe that you need to keep trying to impress your parents, then the wake up call is that train long left the station! You are not thirteen, coming home with your grades. Stand up for who you are, take your power back from your parents' expectations and remember that if anyone's love should be unconditional, it's theirs.

Who ever said being almost perfect was all that awesome anyway?

"We are human beings, not human doings'

Lucy Day, The Modern Medium

Living in a 'have it all' generation, if we look to the media, we are expected to do it all, have it all, be it all. The pressures on us to be perfect are extreme. One such pressure is to always be seen to be 'doing' something — particularly perpetuated by social media, where we feel the pressure to promote all the amazing things we do on a daily basis. Not to mention agreeing to things because we feel we 'should' do them.

Feeling pressured to be constantly on the go and never stopping isn't a virtue, nor is it something to respect or desire. Though we all have seasons of crazy schedules, very few of us have a legitimate need to be busy ALL the time. Being overwhelmed by jobs and deadlines shows that we simply don't know how to live within our means, prioritise properly, or say no when we should.

Being busy rarely equates to productivity these days. Just take a quick look around. Busy people outnumber productive people by a wide margin. Busy people rush everywhere, running late half of the time. They're heading to work, conferences, meetings, social engagements, and hardly have enough free time for family and partners, plus they rarely get enough sleep. Emails fire out of their iPhones like machine gun bullets, and their diaries are jammed to the brim with obligations. A busy schedule gives some of us an elevated sense of importance but it's all an illusion. Do you really want to spend your life like a hamster running on a wheel?

Though being busy can make us feel more alive than anything else for a moment, the sensation is not sustainable long term. You will inevitably, whether tomorrow or on your deathbed, come to wish that you spent less time doing and more time simply being.

Better to have done three things in your day and enjoyed all three than to have achieved twenty-five and wound up stressed and exhausted and having missed out on any joy. When you focus your attention on doing one task well you will find that the task flows far more smoothly and life feels less hectic and pressured.

From today, decide to stop trying to do too much at once. Start saying 'no' more often. In the beginning, you need to say yes to things that will allow you to discover and establish your true self. But as you understand who you are and what you want, you can start to say no, because you know these things won't serve you. Once you know what is the right path for you, what aligns with your true self, focus on doing one thing at a time and doing it well.

If you notice the older generation, you'll see they go pretty slowly! Not just because their bodies are slowed down and they can't fly around everywhere, but because over the years they have learned that taking their time over things makes life so much more enjoyable and that 'doing' is not always the answer. They know a peaceful pace of life brings far greater rewards than rushing.

Slow down. Life is not a race! I can't say this often enough. Reduce your commitments, learn to say no, prioritise your days, don't stack appointments back to back, leave a little space between things you need to do, so you will have room for the unexpected, traffic jams, and so on, etc. Practise the art of 'taking your time' and you'll go through your day much more relaxed.

Decide today that you won't continue to be inefficient simply because you've always done it that way. Start opening your mind to making positive changes and making every day count – that means having periods of work, enjoyment and growth.

If you keep doing what you're doing, you'll keep getting what you're getting. Streamline your life by finding better ways of handling and shortening your to do list.

Take the power back from your obligations and make time to just 'be'. Sitting alone with your thoughts can give your mind a chance to recoup and often start to work creatively and productively.

POWER UP PRACTICE

Are you a list maker? Making lists allows us to free up the energy in our mind and de-clutter all of the 'to dos' that whirl around our heads, keep us awake at night and stress us out all day.

Learn to make a daily list of tasks that need your attention, but also time/date them in order of priority. You'll find that many are not urgent and can be left until tomorrow or later in the week.

Remember to add something to the list which benefits you positively, be it a quick walk, a relaxing bath, five minutes break for a cuppa or (if you're feeling time rich) a massage. Always try to put something positive and uplifting into your day for you and you alone.

Stick today's list here...

The truth does not cease to exist because it is ignored.

- Aldous Huxley

Be Honest

- BE IMPECCABLE WITH YOUR WORD -

Stop meaning what you don't say. Stop saying what you don't mean.

If you ask 100 people what they look for in a partner, it's guaranteed that 9/10 will mention honesty. We all expect honesty from others, but in daily life we tell a hundred lies without realising we're even doing it. From the most basic and common of all conversational lies — 'I'm Fine', and what my Granny used to call 'white lies' which are basically just lies but not big ones, to complex, interwoven lies which are so rooted in untruth that the initiator begins to kid themselves of their honesty and loses grasp of the truth.

Most of us don't lie intentionally and certainly don't lie to hurt others. Quite the opposite in fact, many lies are based on wanting to save another's feelings. But the fact is that for every lie we tell, we lose a little bit of our self-credibility, for we know we have lied and we know it was wrong. No matter how buried our conscience is, it's always there.

When we lie we give power to a false truth, we feel the discomfort of feathering a false reality. It's easy to do but hard to maintain.

The truth will set you free, but it will piss you off first!

Lucy Day, The Modern Medium

Be honest, be kind, be true. If you don't know what to say, just tell your truth. Sure, the truth can hurt, the truth might cause upset or confusion, but it is the truth — it's nothing more than that. When it's out there, there is no further comeback. You don't need to justify it, add to it, remember it or have any concerns. Your truth sets you free.

So what about if there is something that you have done in the past, that you don't wish to be revealed for you worry it could harm a current relationship, or friendship? The fact is, that as long as it remains hidden, you are not carrying out that relationship with a firm base of honesty and truth. For as long as you worry that your 'secret' can be revealed, your power is given over to this possibility and you lose control, allowing fear and worry to reign.

It's not the revealing of your actions that should concern you, but whether you fully own them and whether you are able to release the truth. Rather than wait fearfully for it to be revealed, own up and confess. It happened, you may not be proud of your role in it but if you were responsible for it, take ownership, admit your error to yourself, choose to learn from what happened, stand in your own power and speak the truth.

This may be one of the bravest things you have ever done. Releasing the truth and accepting the consequences, putting your hand up and admitting to wrongdoing, it's all life changing. It may create temporary discomfort but it puts your personal power firmly into your hands creating long-term freedom. It allows you to feel real courage, strength, and moral conviction and illustrates real learning. It shows you that you can grow and benefit from mistakes, because you can right your wrongs.

That doesn't mean you have to broadcast it from a tower, but to those whom you care about, it's so important to be honest.

If you choose not to reveal it, then you leave it there to fester, wrapped in your fears, to be revealed at any time. For there is one guarantee – the truth is always set free, maybe not today, but one day it will be revealed and when that day comes, you must be ready to own it.

Start communicating clearly. Don't try to read other people's minds, and don't expect other people try to read yours. Just be honest. Most problems, big or small, within a family, friendship, or business relationship, start with poor communication and someone holding back, covering up or making something up.

We often say what we think others want to hear, or what we think we need to say to prevent arguments or problems for ourselves. But when we have to put action behind our words and back ourselves up, this is when we come unstuck.

There are only two options — to tell the truth or to say nothing. Of course there are instances when saying something would be damaging, pointless or would stir the pot. Being truthful is about being kind, to yourself and others by not hiding things, lying or making false statements in order to avoid future fall outs. It has nothing to do with judging others, commenting on people's lives inappropriately or telling people what to do. The truth doesn't need to be thrown out into the world like an erupting volcano. However, when there is no choice to keep silent, don't lie — tell the truth.

Don't confuse your truth with other people's beliefs. Just because something feels right to you, true to you, it doesn't mean that you should use it to change other people's beliefs. We all have free will and even if we feel someone else would be happier living in our truth, we must remember that we are not here to preach. If someone asks for our help, then we must always help and offer our advice, but otherwise we are not here to force our truths onto others.

This is especially important when reading books like this. Read with an open mind and heart but only take up the lessons that you truly align with – parts that feel right to you. Don't believe everything everyone tells you. A touch of scepticism is healthy!

Create your own truth.

When you live a life aligned to honesty and truthfulness, there is nothing to remember to say, nothing to fear coming out and nothing to have concern about revealing. You can breathe easy, sleep soundly and know that your conscience is clear. There is nothing more empowering that living in pure honesty.

When you are living in pure authenticity, your outside is the same as your inside – you are the one and only, unique, 100% authentic and completely certified you. Nothing hidden, no surprises, take me as you find me. We love openness and honesty in others – so be the person you would like to meet. Be the change you seek.

POWER UP PRACTICE

Have you seen the film 'Liar Liar' where a man is hypnotized into always telling the truth? Well we're going to play a little game along the same lines. Will you take a challenge in the name of personal power reclamation? Yes? Great!

For the next 24 hours, you must tell the truth and nothing but the truth. Remember that this is not about judging others, or telling people what to do. This is purely about responding honestly when asked questions or considering situations.

This means every question from truthfully answering a simple 'how are you?' at the supermarket, to open and honest discussions with your friends or family at the end of the day.

Enjoy the process. Let your truth open you up, connect you to others and allow peace to flood your heart.

Trust me, you'll love it so much you might just take it up as your new happy habit.

yesterday's the past, tomorrow's the future, but today is a gift. that's why it's called the present.

- Bill Keane

Live in the Moment

We all have a story. We all have history. Some of our stories are so unbelievable they wouldn't make a credible work of fiction, others are pretty steady and normal with the odd drama thrown in.

However exciting, hideous or complicated our past, we seem to have a hankering for it, our minds love to drag us back there, reminding us where we have come from, why we are the way we are, why we can't do what we want to, why we are so bloody screwed up.

But honestly, what is the point of holding onto something that has passed, never to be changed, improved or erased? It is what it is, that was our life and it doesn't mean that it will dictate our future.

It doesn't matter why you did something in the past, or didn't do something. The past is gone, over, ended. The only thing that matters is what you can do right now and how you approach your future.

It doesn't matter if you were a mess, or a complete success. What matters is your attitude going into the next stage of your life. You have nothing to prove to anyone but yourself, all you have to prove is that tomorrow can be happier than yesterday and that you can do whatever it is your heart desires.

All limitations on your life exist solely in your mind

Lucy Day, The Modern Medium

There's no time for regrets, excuses, explanations and reasons. Your backstory is not important now, even if it's brilliant! What is the point on focusing on the past and the why when all we have is the here and now?

Giving power to your past means you have nothing for the present — it leaves you powerless. If your past was tough and you give your power to it, you will never achieve the happiness you seek for your future.

You can't change what happened yesterday but you can ruin today and limit tomorrow by worrying about it. Tomorrow will reveal itself in all its glory if you have your power back in your hands and start with a clean slate.

So learn from your past, take the lessons, try to avoid reliving the same mistakes and then let go. Who you are is not defined by what you have experienced — attitude takes care of that.

What's that? You think it's easier said than done to walk away from your past? Well, it all depends on your perspective. When something difficult happens in your life, you can see it as an opportunity — to learn something about life that you didn't know. It's an opportunity to see how strong you can be in the face of adversity.

Is it really that important? A great tool I find for deciding how impactful and important a situation or decision is, is to consider whether it will be of interest, value or impact in the next 5 years. For example, if I am stressing over whether to go one supermarket or another, I realise that I'm being ridiculous — in five years time I definitely won't be remembering that time I decided to go one supermarket over another and it won't impact my future to any degree! So I pull my power back into my mind and just make the decision, like ripping a sticking plaster off — quickly!

Conversely, big decisions like whether to start having a family now, which house to buy, what job to choose, whether to move areas and so on will all have an impact on your future in five years time and so do deserve some time and effort to resolve.

"When my first child was born, I tried everything in the book to make her sleep but although she wasn't the worst I have come across, she was pretty hard work. It was not uncommon for me to take her for a drive 2-3 times a day just to make sure she had a nap. Sleep kind of ruled my life for a good year or so — it dictated every hour of my day.

Other people seemed to have babies who loved their sleep, but mine was slow to this theory. Whilst she eventually slept through the night, she still made the days hard work.

Pregnant for the second time, I spent quite a lot of time worrying about how I was going to manage organising sleep for another baby with a toddler in tow. I worried about how I'd cope with sleepless nights and the two of them, and how long I would struggle with her sleep for. I was really not looking forward to sleep ruling my life again.

When number two came, she was like a revelation. She slept fairly well from almost day one and was sleeping through the night 50% of the time from only seven weeks old. At nap time she went to bed awake and fell asleep when she wanted to — no crying, nothing! I did nothing different to how I'd raised my first, except I was naturally more relaxed and capable (it is far easier second time around). Sure, we had bad nights, but they weren't half as bad as I had imagined they would be. And, once you're in it, you cope far better than you think you will.

So, my fears had been unfounded.

When I look back, all I see is a waste of energy and concern. I had truly looked to my future through a veil of past experience. I had assumed it would be the same again. But of course just because that's how it has been, doesn't mean that's how it will be again.

A great lesson learned for me there. Now, whenever I find myself donning the 'veil of the past' and allowing my imagination (for that is all fear is, after all) to take over, I stop and put the veil away. Instead I think this time, it will be different. It could be better. Why not?"

Lucy, 36, Australia

There are some days when we all want the day to end and allow us to just crawl into bed and have a good cry. The enormity of responsibility or the pain of regret or simple exhaustion can really knock the stuffing out of us. But it's totally normal to have really crap days where you have no motivation, will power or even care anymore.

It's funny how a rubbish day can feel like a rubbish life; how we can blow up an emotion to such a size that we feel literally like we are dealing with a life or death situation.

This too shall pass

old adage

The trick to overcoming tough times is to drag your power back and slap yourself with the reality that you're just having an awful day, month (or year!) and that this too shall pass! If there's one thing we can be 100% sure of in our existence, it's that time moves on. Nothing stays the same and change is inevitable in the end, whether we create it or not.

Life will look either marginally or completely different in the morning, so when you're having a shocker, try to tread as lightly as you can, stop analysing and trying to make decisions and then fall into bed and just sleep on it.

How different it looks in the morning depends on whether you are moving forward in general, whether you are living within the life you desire or not. If you have already put the wheels of motion to your changes then an awful day is just that. If you are procrastinating and haven't started those changes yet, then your horrible day might just hang around until you start to take control and do something about your life.

Every day in this lifetime counts. So stop wasting time and get on with the job of enjoying it. Today will soon be yesterday and tomorrow will be here before you know it.

Keep your eye on the destination but remember to take frequent breaks to smell the roses. It's a marathon, not a sprint.

POWER UP PRACTICE

THIS TOO SHALL PASS

Write the words above in the middle of a sheet of paper. Around it, briefly write about something in your life that you really love.

Knowing that this situation will pass one day, how does that make you feel about it? ....

Does it make you feel the need to make the most of what you have?
....

Now, next to the words, write briefly about a difficult situation you are facing.

This situation will not be forever, this too shall pass. How do you now feel about it now? ....

Remember, there is light at the end of the tunnel. All we have is now, but change is inevitable. How you deal with, respect and appreciate the NOW will make a fundamental difference to your life. Whatever pain or pleasure you face right now, it will not last forever, this too shall pass.

When you've finished, throw the paper away – remember that not everything you think or write has to be kept, recorded and made sacred. Thoughts come and go and learning develops silently in the background as you go about your daily choices and decisions. You don't need to keep the evidence of where you have been to know that you're growing and developing positively.

we must let go
of the life we
have planned,
so as to accept
the one that is
waiting for
us.

- Joseph Campbell

Learn to Let Go

-LOSE YOUR LIMITATIONS -

In life, you have to learn to make your own sunshine. Happiness doesn't come easily and some hurdles in life are too difficult to clear simply by adopting a positive mindset. I know I have days where I read those positive quotes online and just want to throttle the author — it's not that easy!

But truly, when you step back from your negative mindset, it is. You've just got to want it enough and be willing to work for it. You can't rely on 'luck' to change your world.

If you want to benefit from maximum personal power, drop the disempowering concept of 'luck'. If you truly believe that some of us are luckier than others, you will remain disabled by the possibility that luck will come along and save you. Do you really believe that some people are 'the chosen ones' selected by an invisible power to have a better, richer or more fulfilling life than you? Winning the Lottery is not about luck, it's based on mathematical probability – the numbers you choosing eventually coming up. Marrying someone who seems like the perfect partner isn't about luck, it's finding someone whom you are compatible with, working at staying together and, as we already know, there is no such thing as 'perfect'.

When you instil in yourself the understanding that you create your own happiness, your own compatibility, your own opportunities to 'win' only then do you reclaim that vital personal power and start living the enjoyable life that YOU CREATE for yourself.

One of the greatest disappointments in life is the realisation that your childhood dreams didn't come true just because you wished really hard. It's easy to be twelve and announce that you're going to marry Prince Charming at twenty five, have two kids by twenty eight and be a millionaire living in a country pile by the age of thirty. But earning all that cash, finding 'the one' and popping out a perfect family is a little less easy than your twelve-year-old self realised! Life can be really tough and the responsibilities that come with being an adult can be so uncomfortable that we wish we could be twelve and feel how it is to be a carefree, dependent child again.

OK, so 'millionaire by the age of 30' might have been a bit far fetched but you know what? You're still here and still kicking and you've got a whole lot of life experience under your belt.

Letting go is a hugely important part of taking your power back. Whether it's letting go of a failed relationship, letting someone you love go, or simply letting go of false ideals of how life 'should' be, letting go is fundamental.

Let go of what should have been or could have been. Embrace what is and what will be. There are so many wonderful things in your future for you to expend your energy on, don't allow those things that don't serve you to use it all up. You'd be amazed how much energy goes into negative emotions — what a waste.

Letting go isn't just about releasing the past, or past expectations, or even our preconceptions of what life should have been like by now, it's about shedding everything and anything that doesn't serve us — all negative emotions, habits and actions.

So many of us go to our graves sad and bitter, because we have held loss and lack in our hearts. Living with loss and regret in your heart is completely disabling, leaving you with absolutely no control over your future happiness.

When you let go, you gain your power. You make space in your heart for peace and happiness. You clear the recesses of your mind of what doesn't need to be there and open up to positive, useful thought processes.

If there is any part of you that holds hate, jealousy or dislike in your heart – let it go! Keep your sights set on the future. Holding on to hate and anger is like grasping hot coals with the intent of throwing them at someone else — you are the one who gets burned.

If you want to forget someone or something, and move on, you must give up hating. For as long as you retain any feeling towards them, you are feeling and therefore, you're not letting go. It's hard to forget someone you hate, because hate takes pieces of your heart, thereby keeping this person in there. If you want to forget them, let go of the hate, and create peace in your heart instead.

Also, remember that whenever you hate something, it usually hates you back — people, situations, and inanimate objects alike — which will only further complicate your life.

Letting go releases your problems by releasing their relevance to you — you no longer have to identify with such pain, shame or regrets. Every single issue that you face will give you a chance to practise letting go and being free and the more you do it, the more your power builds back up.

It is so upsetting to watch a bereaved friend lose someone they love and then never let go of the grief that surrounds their loss, but it happens all the time. It's as if their hearts just cling to the memories in sadness, believing guiltily that if they remember too happily, they're not doing the memory or person justice. We're conditioned to mourn.

When it comes to someone who has passed, the very best thing we can do is celebrate their life and let go of the grief. I believe that when we hold them in our hearts in grief and sorrow, this negative energy flows from us to their soul, binding them to Earth, and ourselves, negatively. When we celebrate their life, we send positive, light energy which allows their soul to fly free of the chains of human suffering.

By letting them go energetically, I believe you give them a happier time at rest. It doesn't mean they will not still be around you, or be there for you, but it just means they are free and at peace and in turn, so are you.

Freedom is the ultimate power replenishment so embrace it and fling yourself open to what will be. Enjoy how it feels to be completely unrestrained. Let it go.

POWER UP PRACTICE

Grab a small object that will fit into your hand, something that isn't fragile.

Hold it in your hand, arm outstretched. Now let go of it. Watch it fall to the floor. Pick it up and hold it in your hand again, arm outstretched. Let it roll around your fingers.

Realise that you are holding onto this object, just like you hold onto the past, to fears, to regrets, to pain, to shame, to guilt. You are in control. You choose when to let go.

Now open your hand and let go of the object, drop it. Watch it fall to the floor. You just let go. You are in control. You have the power over your mind. You dictate your actions. You are in the Captain's seat. This is your journey. You choose what and when to release.

Practise this exercise metaphorically and physically. Think about something you hold on to in your mind, hold the object and as you allow it to fall, drop the issue from your mind. Practise this frequently enough to make it really sink in and enjoy the process of metaphorically, mentally and physically letting go.

respect yourself and others will respect you.

- Confucius

Focus on Respect

- NOT POPULARITY-

Facebook has a lot to answer for. Remember in the early days when people used to compare how many friends they had? It was all about quantity and not quality back then. It didn't matter if we had only met someone once, or never even met them, we friend requested and accepted all over the place.

Then after a while, we started to realise that maybe having five hundred random friends reading all about our lives wasn't all that awesome and that five hundred random people's lives weren't all that interesting either. So, slowly, we started to cull a few until we ended up with a still exaggerated but more realistic collection of online friends.

Popularity has been a goal of most of ours ever since school. If you've ever been in the 'uncool' group then you'll know exactly how motivating it is to want to be accepted and admired.

Even in the business world we are told that popularity is important, you just need to look at celebrity to see how popularity makes money. But does it make you happy?

Some people will do anything to be popular, to have followers, people look at them. They will actively seek any type of attention as long as people are looking in their direction.

When we think of fame, beyond the thin veil of money and celebrity, we see people surrounded by sadness and emptiness. There is such a lack of connection, of truth, depth and integrity in the ideal of popularity. There is such an expectation to keep up, to remain a certain way in order to retain followers.

When you give your personal power over to your popularity, you start to rely on it. As soon as you begin to slip off that pedestal a little, you lose not only a little popularity, but also a little control.

Up there in your ivory tower of popularity, you are not you, you are what your followers think you are. No one can truly know you and what it is like to live in your world. All they know is the image that you project. So, in many ways, when you seek popularity, for people to like you, you are creating an image that you think will attract them.

The danger with wanting to be liked, or even admired, is that you then can't cope with not being liked, so you start to do whatever you need to do to be held in favour. This can be as simple as how you act within a circle of supposed friends. You might not really even have anything in common with someone, or have any real reason to be friends with them, but out of the desire to be liked, you still strive to have their friendship, no matter what it takes.

Worrying about what others think of you all the time does nothing but put the power over your happiness into their hands. Whether they like you or not is then the control they have over you – knowingly or not.

Simply be you.

If someone likes you for you, then they are worth having in your life. If you have to work extra especially hard to keep them in your life, then they are not worth it.

This works within business as well. Attract customers, clients and followers who like you and your brand. Unless you have a huge advertising budget, don't seek to educate, preach to the converted.

Seek respect, not attention. When you are earning others' respect, you know you are being true to your integrity and you are sending out a message that others respect. Respect lasts longer than attention and is far more useful in the end. Live a life that makes a difference, one that is effective and impactful, not flashy and impressive for all the wrong reasons. Seek to inspire, not impress.

Anyone who likes you for your car, your house or your title, even your accomplishments, is a trophy hunter and the power has been given to your 'things'. They are not real friends. Don't seek to impress with your adornments, for if there ever comes a day that you are stripped of them, then you will lose all personal power as well as watching their quickly departing backs.

What you have means nothing but who you are and how you live your life means EVERYTHING.

Genuine relationships come from being able to be yourself 100% with someone and knowing that they like you for the real you. You'll form genuine relationships only when you are yourself, all the time. Plus, you'll have a whole lot more energy to spend on the people who count.

Be honest with yourself and everyone else. Don't cheat. Be faithful. Be kind. Do the right thing! It is a less complicated way to live. Integrity is the essence of everything successful. When you break the rules of integrity you invite serious complications into your life. Keep life simple and enjoyable by doing what you know in your heart is right. Be true, be YOU.

POWER UP PRACTICE

Remember your list of values from Strategy 13? Read through the list and apply each one to how you are currently leading your life.

Be honest! Are you embracing your values, living a life in line with them, each and every day? Are you making choices which align with these values?

If you wish to be authentic, to align to your very soul, the central part of you which tries to guide you morally, ethically, emotionally and practically, then it's time to bring your values to the forefront on your existence.

These values are who you are inside, who you are trying to get back to being. Use them as your boundaries and guides and be as authentic as you can.

when you are content to be simply yourself and don't compare or compete, everyone will respect you.

– Lao Tzu, Tao Te Ching

Leave the Competition

-WALK YOUR OWN PATH -

The minute you compete with others, you have given away your personal power — your happiness now depends on whether you do better or feel equal to someone else. Sometimes you will win, but sometimes you won't and if you are hell bent on winning, then boy, will you crash and burn when you lose. Of course if you're an athlete and run competitively for a living, then competition will be essential, but for the rest of us competition normally exists between friends, and that's just not healthy.

As soon as you decide to live your own life and stop worrying about whether you are doing as well as, or better than the next person, your personal power will come snapping back to you and you will find life so much more pleasurable.

Comparing what you have, or what you do, or where you go or how you live is tiring and fruitless. There will always be someone out there who has more, does more, earns more, goes on holiday more and generally seems to be doing better than you, from an outsiders' perspective. And that of course is all it is, for you can never compare your mental state to theirs. You can never truly know how life is for someone else unless you walk in their shoes.

It's not about whether their possessions make them happy, or whether their life is perfect — that is immaterial. What matters is that you don't compare yourself anyway. Of course many of us illustrate and elaborate on our seemingly perfect lives, playing out the detail online in social media groups, but nothing is ever perfect. Many selectively choose which photographs they want to portray their lifestyles and leave out the negative, dull or plain uninteresting. Keeping up appearances has never been more in fashion.

Competition or jealousy can run far deeper and be far more sinister than just trying to keep up, or feeling crap about others' success. I've come across many people in my life who feel better when a close friend is suffering or in need, as it makes them feel elevated — more superior in a way, like they are slightly 'above' in the success game. Few will ever admit to feeling this way but it's rife.

"I have a friend who always seems to be unhappy when I'm happy! If we're chatting online and I have some good news to share with him, he starts to reply in negative and dismissive short messages and then stops writing altogether and goes missing for a few weeks. Then, if I'm struggling or a bit down, he contacts me every day, asking me how I am and we have long, moaning conversations, almost like a competition as to whose life is worse. It's like he's comfortable being friends with me when I'm down but outwardly hates to think I'm ever doing better than him."

Paul, 34, New Zealand

Resentment comes hand in hand with jealousy and sucks up a huge amount of mental energy, energy that could be far better applied in a positive direction. Plus, jealousy is such an uncomfortable emotion, isn't it? It's horrible to feel so rubbish about yourself when comparing to others, it does nothing positive for you all, it just sets you back, making you feel useless and self pitying.

Success and happiness isn't in limited supply — it's abundant and infinite. There is no reason why you can't join those that you admire, rather than compete with those you envy.

If a friend does something amazing, that doesn't mean you can't do something equally amazing in your own eyes. Life is so much more fulfilling when you refuse to resent amazing people or amazing situations and simply celebrate them. The more open you are to incredible, the more you will draw it towards you and realise how much closer to it you are than you think. Enjoy celebrating others' successes too; there's a blessing to be found in shared joy.

You know that the media doesn't help how you think, how you feel that you have to 'have' in order to be truly living. And you also know that the feeling of wanting something is far more potent than having it. You might have lusted after a 'lucky' friend's new handbag until it started to haunt your dreams, but when you eventually get it, the shiny-ness only lasts for a few hours, or days at the most. Then you'll move onto the next thing. Momentary pleasure is fine when it doesn't come at a price. Plus, during the whole process you've given your power, your happiness over to 'having a handbag'. Silly really.

Stuff really is just stuff, and it has absolutely no bearing on who you are as a person. Most of us can make do with much less than we think we need. Take your power back from 'having' and competing and start to concentrate on meaningful connections and experiences.

What is real is your life, your friends and your family, your loves, your highs, your lows, your plans, your fears, not what you see on television and read in the magazines — that's all geared to trying to sell you something, marketing spin and nonsense.

So often we hear 'you need this, you need that' but at the end of the day, we come into this world with nothing and we leave with nothing.

"A few months ago, I was clearing out my late Father's wardrobe. It was piled high with beautiful, hardly worn suits, shirts, shoes and ties. Nobody in the family wanted any of it because nothing fitted them. So the whole lot was going to charity, which I know is good in itself, but it really shouted at me 'you can't take it with you'. All that hard work and money spent on 'things' and at the very end, they are meaningless, nothingness.

What my Father did leave behind was love, people who cared about him so much, memories, experiences, a life lived to the full. He never competed with anyone; he lived his life in his own way, without a care in the world of who liked him, who he was competing with or who he was keeping up with. He did his own thing in his own way. He lived his own life and left a legacy of love. "

Leigh-Anne, 28, U.K.

Take your power back from 'wanting' and apply it to enjoying. Enjoy your life, enjoy your time on Earth. Have quality experiences of your own and sod what everyone else is doing. Care less about what everyone else thinks about you and more about what YOU think.

Truly rich people are those who have a life surrounded by love, who live in alignment with their values, desires, wants and interests, who have freedom in their hearts and peace in their minds.

Truly rich people take charge of their personal power.

They need less to be happy. Wealth is not measured by what you have in your house, but by what you have in your heart. So take the power back and manage your material needs, make money work for you, don't be a slave to your finances.

POWER UP PRACTICE

The next time you hear about a friend's success, take the time to write them congratulatory note/message about it. Share in their happiness and/or success and be a part of their celebration. Sprinkle kindness like confetti.

It's so empowering to leave the competition and join the happiness revolution.

you can't save
a damsel
if she loves
her distress.

- Gossip Girl

Turn your back on Drama

So you know the only person you can change is yourself. And you've decided whether to accept your life or make a change.

No matter how lightly you choose to tread through life, no matter how you try to concentrate on you alone and ignore others, there's always something that crops up and destroys your peaceful little bubble.

Whether it's a family drama, a fight between friends or someone at work who gets your back up on a daily basis, something is always going on.

You could be having a fantastic morning and then one single email pings into your inbox and destroys your calm instantly. You could be sitting chatting to friends, when a harmless conversation about a mutual friend turns into a slanging match that you can't help but join in on.

Did you forget that this is chapter 21? By now, you are the master of your own destiny! You have complete power over what you are involved in and get affected by!

Ever witnessed a friend creating more drama for themselves, simply to take the focus off the real problem? It's like watching a car crash unfolding and we have all done it at some point. There's something enticing about creating a new issue, to remove the emphasis on what we should be choosing to highlight and change for the better. However creating a new drama or focusing on someone else's drama just complicates your life, thrusts you into free-fall and chucks your personal power out into the unknown.

At this point in your powering up process, you've learned to appreciate your life for all its reality and have chosen to make positive changes. You've started to make effective, positive decisions and have shed past fears and worries. You no longer compare yourself to others and have empowered yourself by taking full responsibility for your life.

So why would you now allow drama to add turbulence to your journey? Think about it. Drama only enters into your life when you invite it, therefore you only get involved by choice. EVERYONE has a choice to walk away. It doesn't mean you don't care, it means that you care enough not to try to change someone else's situations, to give them the space to sort out their own problems.

Even when it's your problem, it is you who has the power to accelerate it into a drama or not. It is something that is happening outside of you until you whip it up into a panicked frenzy, swallow it down and make it more than it is. Take the energy and worry away from a situation and what have you got? A situation that can be diffused, managed and solved with time, objectivity and a logical approach. Nothing is unsolvable. Nothing is too big for you to handle, without drama.

Amazing things happen when you distance yourself from negativity — you allow space in your life for positivity, joy and enlightenment. You start to see the beauty in everything, you sleep easier, you find peace faster and life feels so much lighter.

Who needs drama? Not you.

POWER UP PRACTICE

Remember these key rules for breaking out of the drama habit and reclaiming that valuable personal power:

- Walk away from drama, gossip and verbal slanging matches.

- Speak only good about people you know.

- When you know you're swapping one problem for another, switch your focus back and resolve the main issue. More drama is not what you need right now.

- Treat others the way you would like to be treated — start a positivity revolution.

- When a situation threatens to unhinge you, take a step back. Stop the panic from bubbling up and give it an hour before you reply.

- Take the focus off those who refuse to support you. Take your personal power away from them and bring it back to you. It's as simple as that.

CUT OUT & KEEP

it's not how much we give but how much love we put into giving.

- Mother Teresa

Give More than you Receive

The more we wish for, the more power we give away. We base our happiness on having and not giving. It's a negative spiral of frustration when we don't get what we want.

But giving? Well that's a completely different scenario, when you give you don't give away power, you give away love. The more love you give out, the more love you will receive.

Of course the worse practice of giving is one where you expect something in return, from as much as a gift in return note to as little as a thank you. Never give to receive, not even to receive acknowledgment. Just give.

"I used to refuse to give money to homeless people because I hated the thought of them spending my hard earned cash on drugs or drink. Well, that was until I met 'Dave'. Dave was sleeping rough on the streets in Manchester with his dog, Rocky. Rocky was a beautiful Staffordshire Terrier, so loyal to his owner and such a gentle dog. Dave told me that he'd been on the streets for five years and that in that time he had been addicted to drugs. He seemed pretty ashamed to admit it but also said that it was so scary on the streets at night

that taking drugs was an escape — it freed him from the long, frightening nights and numbed the pain.

I saw Dave and Rocky in the same doorway a few times after that meeting and bought him some food and a few drinks. But he'd got me thinking. Who was I to dictate what the homeless man on the street did with my money? As soon as I gave the money to him, it was his money. He had power over his own choices and if he chose drugs, well then so be it. I realised that by giving without condition, without concern for where 'my' money was spent, I was truly giving freely and to give freely was far more empowering for both of us.

Nowadays, if I have enough money in my wallet, I will give it to someone on the streets. I don't know their story, nor do I need to, I know that if I can help in a small way by giving without condition or expectation, I will."

Laura, 39, Sydney, Australia

When you give without condition, you retain your power and ensure you don't take someone else's. Saying a kind word, nodding a hello, smiling at someone on the street, giving a thank you card, taking a present for a friend, offering your help, however big or small, giving to others makes you happy. It takes the focus off you and allows you to release love to someone who might really need it.

In this world, there are givers and there are takers. The takers will never be happy, for they will always wonder what's in it for them, the givers will be free.

Holding out on people means you really hold out on yourself.

Quite simply, give what you want to receive. If you want love, give love. If you want friends, be friendly. If you want money, provide value.

If you spend any time online, you will have heard of the new practice of 'Random Acts of Kindness', which is basically the art of giving to a stranger, or someone you know for no reason at all — randomly. There are many stories of strangers doing kind things, giving surprise presents, support or letters, to make others feel good or to help in some way for absolutely no recognition or return.

Random Acts of Kindness don't just make great stories, they make the receiver's heart sing and the giver's energy soar. When you give without expectation of anything in return, you give with a truly free heart. To give to a stranger takes the levels of expectation to an extreme level.

There are so many ways to participate in a random act of kindness, from 'paying it forward at a café' – which basically means leaving enough money at the till for the next person in line to receive their coffee/cake for free, to leaving a 'love bomb' – which is a motivating, inspiring note left somewhere random for a stranger to pick up and benefit from, to simply doing something kind for someone in need.

RAOK (Random Acts of Kindness) are like a love virus, spreading across the world. They are the antithesis of terrorism, the opposite of terror and horror, they spread the hope that no matter what kind of shit you're dealing with, there is always someone out there that cares, even a complete stranger.

The buzz you will get from giving a RAOK is secondary to the kindness and love you spread, but it will be palpable and it is infectious! Enjoy the moment that your heart opens and your soul connects to another in the most selfless, purest and briefest of ways.

There's loads of inspiration on Love Bombing and RAOK on the web, but for me, the best love comes from your heart, unique to you and your motivation. Maybe next time you get a chance to give to a stranger, you will.

POWER UP PRACTICE

Find an opportunity to practise a RAOK this week. Whether it's a kind note left on the table of a busy train, leaving enough change at a coffee shop for the next person to enjoy their coffee for free, or simply helping someone across the road, or to their car with their bags, or opening a door for a stranger.

No matter how big or small, make sure it's random, kind and thoughtful. You will love doing it and benefit so much from the lack of requirement to receive thanks, a response or a reward. The act of giving will be a huge reward in itself.

The weak can never forgive forgiveness is the attribute of the strong.

— Mahatma Gandhi

23

Forgive Others

Normally when I broach the subject of forgiveness with my clients, I am met with hesitation. By forgiving their perpetrator, they feel they are condoning their wrongs. I always say that to forgive, you don't have to agree with their ways, like them or condone them. You have to forgive them. Forgiveness leads to freedom and the most beautiful ascension from pain, it opens your wings and allows you to fly.

Forgiveness frees up not the other person, but you. Holding resentment and anger in our hearts poisons us, making it hard for us to move on and love others freely.

By forgiving, it doesn't mean we are accepting or condoning the other person's actions, it means that we are letting go of them and not allowing them to affect us any more.

Forgiveness doesn't make you weak, it makes you free

Lucy Day, The Modern Medium

We all have experiences in our past where we've been left with a bitter taste in our mouths by someone we felt negative towards. For some of us, that distaste manifests as resentment or hatred.

If you imagine yourself as a ball of energy (which I believe you are) then the energy that you put into hating and not forgiving someone, anyone, is a string of energy flowing constantly from you to them.

Now imagine that energy as your personal power. There is a string of personal power that constantly flows to that person. Whether you never see them again, or have to spend every day with them, the energy will continue to flow anyway.

When you decide to forgive, you don't agree to forget and nor do you condone, but you do release yourself from negativity.

Firstly you must accept that no words are going to make the difference here. This is not about talking it out or working through it with the other person. For pure forgiveness all you need is to want to be free of the negative emotion.

Next you seek to understand. Now, this doesn't mean you have to agree with the other person's actions, but you understand then from their point of view.

"My Dad was pretty disappointing, in fact he was a really poor example of a Dad. He never remembered birthdays, was selfish and self centred and all we seemed to do was fall out. When he left me and Mum to start a family with his new girlfriend I would go for weeks, even months without hearing from him. I don't think he really ever cared that much for me. Looking back our relationship really damaged me when all I really wanted was for him to show he cared.

Some years later I realised that despite getting on better with him as an adult (and keeping him at arm's length) I hadn't forgiven him for his rejection of me as a child. It took me a long time to finally decide that life was too short and I needed to make peace with my feelings about him. So, on the advice of friend, I didn't tackle him about our past, instead I sought to understand him. When I thought about his background, the fact his Dad had left when he was only ten and the difficult upbringing he had, I realised that rejection kind of ran in his blood. He didn't grow up with a male role model in his life and he hadn't learned how to turn that around for his own kids. I also realised that despite his achievements in life, he had never really been happy. He seemed to have chased money, popularity, success but never really felt content with his lot. He was also innately selfish.

I didn't like it, but I understood it. I could see why he had been so offhand and why he had actively avoided being a parent of a teenager. I pretty much figured his problems were rooted in a life of discontent and fear.

So, I worked really hard to forgive him. Not to agree with him, but to let it go. After months and months of repeating it to myself, I finally started to believe it. Now, I feel no resentment towards him, just love. I know he was a crap Dad and he did hurt but I don't let it define our relationship. And you know what, I have learned where he didn't. I work really hard to make sure that my kids don't experience rejection, that I am the Dad that he wasn't, because after all I realise, he was my teacher — he taught me how to be better.

The best thing that came out of forgiving my Dad was that, despite the fact he had no idea I'd done it, our relationship improved even further. I guess it was a consequence of me being different with him. I started to care more than I had done in years and that must have showed. Sadly, my Dad got very sick just after we reconnected and so now we are unable to speak to each other, but at least I know in my heart, when I think of him, I am at peace."

Jack, 41, London, U.K.

Forgiveness is a promise you want to keep. When you forgive someone you are making a promise not to hold the unchangeable past against your present self. It has nothing to do with freeing a criminal of their crime and everything to do with freeing yourself of the burden of being an eternal victim.

My proven methodology for forgiveness requires two minutes of effort every day. The only real requirement is that you have to want it. You can't do it without really meaning it otherwise it doesn't work. You have to want the freedom that comes with letting go. This means letting go of the story that comes with the lesson.

For an effective exercise in forgiveness, follow these steps:

Find somewhere that you can be quiet and peaceful and alone for two minutes.

Close your eyes and imagine the person you'd like to forgive is sitting in front of you.

Picture them in your mind and imagine showering them in a gold light

In your mind, say to them 'I forgive you and send you love'

Say it ten times.

Then say thank you and let the image go.

The first few times you won't believe it or mean it but to work, you have to do this little exercise maybe fifty times! Every time you get a moment, repeat it.

It's that simple.

By doing something that requires no discussion or meeting or argument or counselling, you are letting go of the past. It's like choosing to increase your altitude and fly higher than everyone who has held you up on your journey.

You accept that this is the present and nothing can change what has happened. You are exerting your own power in the situation and taking charge of your emotions. Remember that holding a grudge hurts nobody but you. Letting go of the actions that made you upset in the first place and letting go of the negative emotions is the key to emotional freedom and the repossession of your power.

Be grateful for every experience you have, every lesson you learn and remember that people are put in your way to test you. They test your strength, your resolve, your morals and your ability to learn. How will you know love if you haven't known the opposite? How will you know happiness if you have never been sad?

Let go of the story, make space in your mind for love and feel the peace in your heart that forgiveness creates. It's worth it, I promise you.

POWER UP PRACTICE

Look up and read the beautiful story called 'The Little Soul and The Sun — A Children's Parable' by Neale Donald Walsch, before answering these questions...

Who has taught you a lesson in forgiveness?
....

How often do you think of them?
....

How has your negativity towards them and their actions prevented you from moving forward?
....

How does your lack of forgiveness affect your day to day development?
....

How will you move forward with this new understanding?
....

➜ Is it time to reclaim your power and your freedom?

friends...
they cherish
one
another's hopes.
they are kind
to one another's
dreams.

- Henry David Thoreau

Choose your Friends Wisely

You will only ever be as great as the people you surround yourself with, so be brave enough to let go of those who keep bringing you down. You don't need to force connections with people who constantly make you feel less than amazing.

As with keeping up with the competition and wanting to be popular, wanting to be liked by everyone is truly a fruitless and powerless task. Imagine giving your personal power over to every person who you befriend! When you allow how others feel about you to dictate your happiness, you are completely out of control.

It's ok to be choosey when becoming friends with someone as long as you don't take it to the extreme. Shyness can be debilitating when it starts to prevent you from meeting others, but to expect everyone to like you is ridiculous. Think of yourself like marmite/vegemite — some people will love you, some won't! But everyone has different tastes and interests — we can't be all things to all men and women.

Similarly, if you feel emotionally drained after spending time with someone or get a small jolt of discomfort when you are reminded of them, listen to your intuition. There are so many "compatible people" for you, who energise you and inspire you to be your best self. It makes no sense to force it with people who are the wrong match for you.

If someone makes you feel uncomfortable and insecure every time you're with them, they're not close friend material.

Like any relationship, having friends takes a little effort on both sides, but having unrealistic expectations of someone else, once again puts the power over your happiness into their hands.

If you want to call a friend but feel like you are the only one who puts the effort in, then don't start to play games and wait for them to call, make a decision about whether you are happy for this to be the way your friendship is, or not. Friendships take many forms and you have the power to decide how prominently each form features in your life.

In the same way that you wouldn't try to change your partner, don't try to change your friends' personalities. Friends accept each other for exactly who they are, warts and all. If you've chosen a crappy friend who is self-centred, unreliable or just not really that great to be with, then it's not for you to try to change them, just decide what you are willing to accept and what you won't.

You don't need to feel guilty about being selective over who you have as a friend, or who you stop spending time with. So many people hate the thought of 'unfriending' someone they have known for a long time, but truly, if your relationship doesn't serve you both positively, what is the point of it? Friends are supposed to be people you look forward to spending time with, not compete with or criticise.

If a friend is causing you discomfort, pain or any negative drama, then cut loose and move on. It sounds harsh, but truly, if the positive energy has left the relationship, then neither of you is making the other happy.

"We are addicted to our thoughts. We cannot change anything if we cannot change our thinking."

Santosh Kalwar

How many times have you allowed your mind to create a huge drama where there was none? Say you text your friend and she doesn't reply for two days, which is very unlike her. Within those 48 hours you will likely have decided that she's fallen out with you, that you've done something terribly wrong. You'll be stressing all over the place until you finally hear from her, only to find out that she had been away with work and called you as soon as she had a moment to herself.

Or maybe a work colleague went off to lunch without you, which was very unlike her. You'll have decided that you've obviously done something to piss her off and will have been asking everyone 'is Sarah ok today? Have I done something to offend her?' Only for her to return from her lunchtime optician's appointment, which she'd forgotten to tell you about.

We can all find reasons to be offended on a daily basis, but look how we can create drama based on nothing but our imagination. Giving away our power to such situations is such a waste of energy and emotion, so unnecessary.

When you assign negative intent to innocent situations, you are taking things personally and being really self-centred. Don't take things personally! Be positive and let go, stop giving others the power over your peace of mind. Look for the good in everyone you meet and give everyone the benefit of the doubt.

Spend time with positive people. Remember that like attracts like. Relationships should help you, not hurt you. Surround yourself with people who mirror the person you want to be. Choose friends who are proud to know you and you are proud to be with, people you like who love and respect you. Choose to be friends with people who make your day a little brighter simply by being in it.

Life is too short to spend time with people who have the power to make you miserable. Be you, and allow like to attract like.

POWER UP PRACTICE

Do you collect friends or make friends?

Think about all those close to you. Who do you work hard at being friends with? Who do you have an easy relationship with? Which of your friends is actually more of an acquaintance? Do you have 50:50 relationships in terms of effort and interest? Who could you not see for a year and still be able to catch up and chat with like it was yesterday?

Remember that friends are not a necessity they are supposed to be a positive addition, a choice.

If it's hard work, it's not friendship. If it makes you sad, it's not friendship. If you don't know where you stand, it's not friendship.

Be more selective, value yourself more and surround yourself with people that make you smile. When it comes to friendships choose quality over quantity.

The easiest path is not always the right one.

- Lucy Day 'The Modern Medium'

Choose the right path

- NOT THE EASY WAY OUT -

You know by now that the thing with deciding to change is that it instils a sense of discomfort in and resistance to the life you are trying to leave. With discomfort comes the desire to get 'the good life' now and with that comes impatience and restlessness. You know that better is out there for you, so you want it right now.

But life is a journey, not a race, and changes that will last you a lifetime take time to make. If the changes you make are rash and reactive, based on short-term issues, you will only get a short-term solution and secondary long-term problems.

Have patience with the process, it takes time to make fundamental changes to your life. Sure, some decisions are really easy to make, once you've decided to go for it. A difficult relationship can be finished in seconds, but the implications of then being alone and making your new lifestyle work for you can take a long time. Instant happiness doesn't exist, or if you do experience it, then it isn't lasting, it's momentary, a fleeting emotion. True, deep down contentment comes with finding your place in life and that can take a lifetime!

Be content with the fact that you have put your intentions out into the world and that you have a plan and you are working on it. Don't rush, trying to make 'your life' come to you quicker. Remember, life is what is going on all around you while you're waiting for it to happen!

This is your life, it's valuable and precious and if you get it right, it can bring you wonders. This isn't time to cut corners. Avoid future headaches by doing things right the first time.

Doing the best at this moment puts you in the best place for the next moment. Why give less than 100%? Life is too short to waste it by living below your full potential. If something is worth doing, then it's worth doing well.

Patience, respect for the process, commitment and effort are what it takes to live the life you want. I often talk of following the light path to your future; for me this is the path of least resistance — the one that allows you to reach your identity, your true self, and your potential with the fewest hurdles. But that doesn't mean that the hurdles won't be there, that there will not be days when you wonder if it's all worth it, when you question your decisions. But know that being the master of your destiny is so worthwhile, when you finally start to feel the benefits of self-control, self-mastery and self-fulfilment.

Don't look for a short cut. Don't cheat yourself. Do the right thing, by you, by other people, by the world. Do the right thing even if no one else will ever know. Why? Because YOU will know. In your heart you will have peace with your decisions and that is priceless.

POWER UP PRACTICE

1. What daily actions can you take to support creating your limitless life? For example:
    - ✓ Eat healthily
    - ✓ Drink enough water
    - ✓ Read, learn and grow
    - ✓ Exercise
    - ✓ Take time out
    - ✓ Mindfulness meditation

Create your own list for today.

2. What should today's affirmation be? Create one for yourself. For example: *I believe in myself and my abilities.*
....

3. What step are you going to take today in pursuit of positive change?
....

4. What three things are you grateful for today?

1) ....
2) ....
3) ....

Adopt the above checklist to set up your daily routine. Just a few lines sets your positive intentions for the day. With your power in tact, start as you mean to go on.

The greatest test of courage on earth is to fear defeat without losing heart.

- Robert Green Ingersoll

26

Be fearless

- RELEASE THE OUTCOME -

You've already practised making decisions based on love over fear, but imagine living a life where you feared nothing. The more we seem to accumulate, in material and energetic wealth, the more we have to potentially lose. As a result, those of us who were fearless teenagers become quite fearful of loss in later life.

Of course there are many natural reasons for accumulating a sense of fear. As mothers, for example, the moment our babies are born, we fear for them so much it hurts. And of course it's natural to fear losing someone we love or loving someone so much that we fear losing their love, but if we take this fear to extremes, we can often create the loss we fear most.

Desperation and fear makes us act differently. We stop letting life flow and start basing our happiness and contentment on maintaining the status quo, keeping everything the same, or accumulating more in the fear of losing it all.

When we give power to our fears, they grow and soon the fear of loss spirals out of control. We refuse to even get in the Captain's seat, let alone take off. We remain static on the runway, too scared to see where the journey will take us in case everything goes wrong and we come plummeting down to earth.

Remember that like attracts like — what we put out we receive.

Fear doesn't stop you from dying, it stops you from living

Lucy Day, The Modern Medium

We all know that life is relatively short, but looking at it as a finite opportunity to truly live is far better than fearing a death that is, quite frankly, inevitable. It's not a coincidence that those who are faced with terminal illnesses suddenly reveal a bucket list of things they would like to do before they pass away. When faced with your mortality, you realise how much life has to offer and have the motivation to get on and do it. Imagine living the rest of your life like you knew you were going to die... Oh yes, that's right, you already do. So what are you going to do today that really shows you are living?

Live your life to the full. Don't ignore death, but don't be afraid of it either. Beware of a life you never lived because you were too afraid to take action. Death is not the greatest loss in life. The greatest loss is what dies inside you while you're still alive. Be bold. Be courageous. Be scared to death, and then do it anyway.

Stepping outside your comfort zone scares you, sure, but the benefits that you get from the strength you gain in pushing yourself out there are infinite. Do something today that makes you feel uncomfortable, something that makes your brain shift out of its habitual processes and forces you to think, to use the intellect you were born with. Make something of your life and take a few risks. What is the worst that can happen?

There are people the world over who have suffered incredible loss, of family, love, security, safety and who have picked themselves off and started again. Loss does not mean the end, it means a requirement to adapt, to get up and try again. Sometimes loss of one part of your life can mean a huge gain in another.

The day after I finished writing this chapter, I sat with a client who was literally scared to death. She feared her life so much that she was projecting her fear into areas of her life where, truly, there was nothing to worry about. As her father, who had passed, stepped into the room in spirit, I understood instantly where her fear stemmed from. She had felt his loss so acutely that she was terrified of losing another family member, losing her husband, her mother, anyone close to her. Her father told me that he had been her sounding board when he had been alive, she had run everything past him. Now he had gone, she was scared to make a decision without his approval.

So I asked him, 'what do you want to tell her?' His response was positive, 'tell her that I am behind her in anything she wants to do. But she knows this, she knows how I would answer. I am so proud of her but she is wasting her talent! She could be so successful and happy, she holds herself back.' He then went on to show me that he had passed very suddenly and that he had regrets about what he had not done with his life. He had lived a fairly steady and risk-free life, but in his heart he had been far more adventurous. He'd not put his desires into action. He also showed me that he was a closet romantic and he wished he had been more romantic with his wife.

My client listened to all of this and I explained to her that her father was giving her a very important message. His passing was a lesson to her.

Not just a lesson in coping with loss but a lesson in learning to live for the moment and realising that this life is finite —there is an end. He was telling her to make the most of the life she had and to make every second count. He didn't want her to go to her grave with regrets.

Hearing this from her father changed this lady's life. She left knowing she needed to change her perspective, feeling that truly, the only person holding her back was her. She took her power back and realised that she needed to face her fears head on.

Take your power back too. Live a life of fearlessness, strength, conviction and challenge. Don't sit back on your laurels and let yourself rot in your fear of failure/change/loss. Nobody said it was easy, but that is the lesson, accessing the inner power and putting it into action, pushing forward despite the challenges.

Living in fear is paralysing and pointless and to be honest, not living at all. When it comes to worrying about losing what you have, you give all your personal power to the things that keep you afloat, whether that be your house, your money, your possessions or your relationship. The pressure you put on yourself to retain it is hard work!

If you've ever suffered heartbreak, you know how hard it is. But you know what? You've been through it, you're experienced now, you know what it feels like and you know the signs that it's coming. It is true that once you heart has been broken, it will never be broken in the same way again. Take another chance on love, this time with your eyes wide open but with a heart full of the same hope for a positive outcome, however aware of what you will and won't accept this time. A broken heart is a wiser one, stronger and more aware. A broken heart knows how much it hurts to be destroyed and so it won't let itself be destroyed in that way again. A broken heart knows loss and sadness, so it won't feel that depth of sadness again. The worst is over. Take your power back and strengthen yourself with the knowledge that now you know, you are aware, you will protect yourself better this time.

Dust yourself off and try again. Don't close your heart for fear of further loss, for the truth is that every minute your heart is closed off, you are losing anyway. You can't feel the amazing depth of emotion that comes with loving and being loved if you have closed off. Empower your heart and open it back up, take the risk and enjoy the benefits.

We are adaptable, we change according to changes in our environment, so trust yourself to cope with whatever life throws at you, if and when it throws it. Don't live under the false protection of fear. Life is for living so do it in the glorious Technicolor that it deserves.

POWER UP PRACTICE

Have you ever written a bucket list? It's a list of things you'd love to do in this lifetime. It doesn't have to be limited to wild and crazy activities, it can include improvements to your career, home life, relationship and friendships.

So what do you want to do? What does your bucket list look like? How does it feel? Have you tried anything on it before? What did you learn from trying?

Write your own bucket list. Be creative, be indulgent, be free and wild and create ideas with abandon. Don't limit yourself, don't hold back, release your needs, desires and wants. Get them all out.

Now…What is getting in the way?

This part requires some work, so enjoy the process and take your time with it. Dig deep to uncover the source of what is needed to make the changes you seek.

For each 'desire' list a couple of reasons why you haven't achieved it yet. Then dig into those reasons and look for the source. For example:

Desire: *To go travelling for three months.*
Blockages: *Not enough money, time off work.*
Solution: *Earn more, take sabbatical.*
Blockages: *Can't get a pay rise in current job.*
Solution: *Seek new position.*
Blockages: *Didn't succeed in last 3 interviews.*
Why: *Because I was over-qualified.*
True Blockage: *Fear of failure. Fear of challenge. Aiming too low – settling.*
Solution: *Take power back, release failure, harness determination, apply for suitable positions. Aim for more challenging positions to suit your experience. Be brave.*

When you break down the desires, you can start to see where you have lost your power along the way. Repeat this for each desire and you will see that many of your desires can be overcome by the exact same root solution. This method illustrates how you can reduce your required changes down to far fewer than you thought you would need whilst achieving far more of your desires than you thought you would!

gratitude makes sense of our past, brings peace for today, and creates a vision for tomorrow.

- Melody Beattie

27

Count your blessings

There's always someone worse off than you. There is always someone suffering a fate that in your experience would be completely unthinkable. In a life where anything is possible, there are some terribly tragic situations on every corner.

Of course sadness is relative and we all feel negativity for different levels of difficulty. What seems like a tragic life to one would be a walk in a park for another. However, to compare our own life to someone else's, no matter whether you see theirs as better or worse, is always a mistake.

Your life is a product of your choices. You have made decisions for years and years that have all culminated in the life that lies before you. Sure, when things are tough all you see is barriers and difficulties, challenges and obstacles, where on a better day you might see opportunities and blessings.

Unless we walk a mile in someone else's shoes, we cannot understand how life is for them. We can't understand how tough it is, or easy. We can only compare what we feel about our life to what we see happening in theirs.

Of course it's all about attitude. Even those in the toughest of situations can find things to be grateful for, no matter how pitiful they may seem to others. The thing with living a life of gratitude is that, once again, what we give out, we receive. When we start to see the beauty in the small things, we start to see that there are more small and beautiful things to appreciate, and more and more, until we start to realise that there is beauty all around us.

We are blessed with the gift of life, and those of us in countries free of war are blessed with the gift of freedom. Our only boundaries and limitations are those that we set for ourselves. There truly is a glass ceiling above our heads, one that we placed there and can quite easily break through.

When we start to see the beauty in the small things, we realise we can only be grateful to one person — to ourselves. Remember that you created the life you have and so if there is anything to be thankful for, you should thank yourself. You are fully responsible for your life exactly as it is, and when you start to make changes to your life to let a little more happiness in, well you did that too.

Gratitude creates a feeling of abundance — of having so much more than we thought we had. Simply having our health is such an empowering situation, for example. So many people cannot live a full life because their poor health holds them back. So, when you have your health, this is something to be incredibly grateful for.

Gratitude can be applied incredibly effectively to the past to create a new story. When we look back at our experiences to find the gratitude within them, we can start to understand why things happened, what lessons were there for us and how well we reacted in those situations. For example, if you had a really tough relationship breakup but you realise that you would never have met your current partner had you not left your ex, you can start to feel gratitude that the breakup happened. For without one loss, the new gain would not have happened. Not to mention the gratitude you can feel for the strength and knowledge you gained during the process. If nothing else, you learned what you didn't want from a relationship and you learned how to value yourself a little more.

Gratitude is a way of life. It allows you to see the beauty in things in front of you as well as behind you. You start to see the benefits, the positive in so many more situations, and you will find that you start to let life flow a little more, rather than hiding in your safe place of fear.

Gratitude is infectious. As soon as you start to feel it, it snowballs. Before you know it, you'll start to feel grateful for all sorts of things. It's the perfect antidote to feelings or concerns about loss. Loss cannot exist when you live in gratitude. Fear cannot exist when you live in gratitude, for gratitude is the ultimate enabler, one of the most empowering feelings you can arm yourself with.

When you live in gratitude, you live in the centre of love. And love heals all. Living a life based in gratitude retains your personal power with ease, sustaining it for the long journey ahead. It anchors your personal power to your core and allows you to envisage the journey for the beauty it will enfold, the joy, the excitement, the wonder and beauty. Gratitude fills your heart with the power of feeling complete every day, feeling content and bathed in the warmth of perpetual appreciation.

POWER UP PRACTICE

Let's practise.

This evening, before you go to bed, count your blessings. Note down three things that you are grateful to yourself for — for example, working hard enough that you put food in your fridge and a roof over your head, for caring about others, for keeping going despite difficulties.

It might be very simple words of gratitude at the start, but after only a week, you will start to become more and more creative with your gratitude. When you get a chance to read all these notes back in the near future, you will be empowered and strengthened by the knowledge of how completely abundant your life truly is.

pray as if god will take care of all; act as if all is up to you.

- Ignatius

Fake it

- 'TIL YOU MAKE IT -

Through the last twenty-seven chapters you have been on a transformational journey. One that has been jam-packed full of positive, personal power practices, inspiration, guidance and advice on how to reclaim your personal power and live a life of inspiration, motivation, encouragement and enjoyment. Of how to become the pilot on that journey — to navigate your own path, take responsibility for your own decisions and empower yourself to ditch the passive attitude of the passenger.

The journey has been simple in theory but perhaps harder in practice. Whilst you have every intention to put these changes into practice, fundamental changes don't happen overnight, and nor should they. This journey is about changing habits that have been cultivated over a lifetime. It takes time for new positive thought processes to sink in and replace the old habits.

So while you are waiting for the changes to take hold, don't get impatient; allow life to ebb and flow whilst you sit in your personal power and enjoy the feeling of being the master of YOUR life.

As the master, you have the responsibility for illustrating your life. It takes time to create a masterpiece, but it will be worth it in the end.

Until the masterpiece is completed, you have two choices — to worry and panic about when you will start to feel better, when life will change. Or, act as if life is exactly as you desire right now — fake it until you make it.

Faking it until you make it is a bit like a dress rehearsal. You get everything in place and then give it a go. You dress up and practise, despite your fears. You may not be confident, you might worry about the outcome but you don't let that worry stop you, you just get up and go. You show up!

If you want to be lucky, you practise feeling lucky. If you want to be happy, you practise feeling happy; if you want to be successful, you practise feeling successful. If you want to be courageous, well, you get the idea.

Of course I'm not referring to pretending to be something you're not, or lying to yourself or other people. This is about practising your new confident attitude now in order to make it a permanent attitude in the future. If you lack confidence in your future, that's OK, pretend you're confident until your true feelings start to match up. Face your fears and do it anyway, but do it with a smile on your face.

If you sit and wait for happiness to find you, it never will. You have to practise being who you want to be, right now.

For example, if you've always dreamed of being a writer but have never shown anyone your work, give it a go! Set up an online blog and start writing about something that interests you. When you feel you have something, anything, worth a little read, share it with a few close friends. By the time you have done this, you are more experienced than you were before you started, and guess what? You're a writer. Not a published one, but an open one — you've embraced the life you want and you've taken the first step on the ladder. It may not be a masterpiece but it's a start, and the courage it took to take that first step is a huge hurdle overcome.

Remember that you're a work in progress, so embrace that feeling! We are all perpetual works in progress. None of us knows it all or has done it all. Being a work in progress doesn't mean you're not good enough yet; it means you want a better tomorrow and you wish to live your life fully. It means you're determined to heal your heart, expand your mind and cultivate the gifts you know are in there.

You've got this.

Time for Take off

You wake after a restful sleep and have a long leisurely breakfast. Checking yourself out in the mirror as you get ready for the trip of your life, you send a nod of gratitude that your body is ready to do this. You feel good.

You stroll out onto the tarmac with a confidence in your step. You may never have done this before, but you're safe in the knowledge that a positive attitude will overcome any nerves.

See that plane over there? That plane is ready, waiting to take you on the journey of your life. No longer do you load your luggage and wait for the pilot to take off. Not this time.

This is your plane, your journey, your destination. You are the pilot and the journey offers you ultimate freedom, nobody can hold you back.

You do the pre-flight checks — accepting your choice of plane, your time of flight, happy with your decisions so far.

As you step into that cockpit and survey all the dials, the pedals, the buttons and panel, confident that this in your plane, you intuitively know what to do — you are in control.

You sit up straight and take hold of the controls. Your eyes widen in excitement at the runway before you, with its promise of pure freedom.

You know your route, the route you alone have chosen to take, the route that suits you perfectly. It's sunny today, but you accept that the outlook might change at any time. You have empowered yourself with the knowledge that you will overcome any inclement weather. You've braved and overcome difficulties before, and you can do it again.

You trust yourself to know when to set off, when to apply the power — to start the journey. You feel the wheels roll beneath you and look into the sky at the promise that lies before you — the potential of the journey you are about to take.

You feel your plane speed across new ground, and you slowly lift your whole being into the thrill of the unknown.

This is it. This is the journey. The wonderful, incredible, fearless journey.

You're doing it.

You are the pilot.

You have the power.

You are the power.

Enjoy every second.

About the Author

It's taken Lucy Day 36 years to drop others' expectations and create her authentic self — she likes what she's made so far. A self-proclaimed 'word-junkie' it was only a matter of time before a book finally clambered out of her and into the world.

Having enjoyed a successful career in business, as the Managing Director of her own pharmaceutical business and as a qualified life and business coach, her truth refused to be silenced and so she left her corporate career to embrace her calling as a psychic medium and life coach.

She's currently pushing her own boundaries as a student pilot and hopes one day to fly her young family across Australia. Her go-to saying is 'this too shall pass' and when she's not giving psychic guidance to clients across the world, or pouring her soul into her laptop, you'll find her dancing around the kitchen to 80s power ballads with a baby on each hip and a smile from ear to ear.

Lucy gives private readings and runs workshops from her practice in Townsville, Australia, and offers distance email and Skype readings to clients all over the world. To connect with Lucy, please visit

www.themodernmedium.com

Thank you!

Thanks for reading! If you enjoyed my book, please add a short review or send me an email and let me know what you thought. I love to receive feedback, insights and personal stories of how you have got on with taking back your personal power – after all the book was created for you (and I love a good chat!)

Your Invitation to The Flight School

If you enjoyed my book and want to make the most of your new mindset, visit **www.themodernmedium.com/flightschool** to reserve your invitation to my exclusive online academy.

The Flight School is designed to relate the life changing strategies from this book directly to YOUR life, CEMENTING your newly found knowledge and ensuring retaining your personal power is EFFORTLESS.

The Flight School membership gives you all the tools you need to make the wisdom in my book really come alive, with daily inspiration, thought provoking videos, personal success stories, empowering workshops, downloadable worksheets and much more.

See you on the runway...

Lucy

Praise for Lucy Day

For latest testimonials visit www.themodernmedium.com

"Hi Lucy, thanks for my reading yesterday. Not only did you "hit the nail on the head" with the issues affecting me at the moment, you've given me some valuable insight on how to move forward. You have an amazing gift that I am so impressed with. Thanks again"

Thank you Lucy. Thank you for today. It was incredible that you knew so much about my situation and could even describe my house and partner's personality and traits. You were so spot on about everything. Thanks again."

"You are such a beautiful, warm & welcoming person. You made me feel instantly at ease & comfortable. I was, and still am, utterly amazed at how you were able to bring out the major issue in my life - especially when I had no preconceived ideas or questions for you. I absolutely appreciate having the opportunity to 'communicate' with mum. I just can't stop thinking about it. You are fantastic. Thank you, thank you. I will definitely be referring my friends."

"Lucy you are truly gifted. I have been to readings before, but you blew them out of the water. You have the most amazing ability. Your insights into my life in 1 hour, was 100 times more valuable then the 10 sessions I had with a counsellor. You gave me clarity, and a firm nudge, to be true to myself to make better decisions, and that, I will always be grateful for. I'm so glad you are willing to share your gift, to enrich others lives. Thank you."

"Thank you for helping me see what paths I need to take to ensure I get the best out of my life. I left feeling like I can go on to achieve what I have always wanted to do career wise. You were spot on about so many things especially with my relationship with my husband and how my life is at the present time. I'm so glad I took the step to have a reading as it has made things so much clearer for me. I look forward to returning sometime in the future to have another reading."

"I just want to say thank you so much for your reading. You were spot on with all information and gave great guidance. I felt amazing after my session. Great energy was felt today. I will definitely be recommending you to any person who is after a little guidance and clarity in their life. It was a such a blessing for you to be able to connect with some of my loved ones also – it gave me such joy."

"Your connection with me was amazing, one of the most accurate readings about my life, my struggles and my future - amazing. You knew the name of the person in question without me mentioning it. Advice, validations & predictions were realistic and spot on too. Big Thank You for my reading. You will be seeing me again!"

"You truly have a gift, thanks so much for sharing it with me! I left feeling so much more at ease and your words and insight have meant more to me than anything else at this time. Such an amazing talent. I have already recommended you to my friends and hope to see you again one day also."

"I would like to say a big Thank You for my reading last week. Your connection with me was amazing, one of the most accurate readings about my life, my struggles and my dreams I have ever had - spot on with all of them. Thanks to your reassuring honesty in telling me what I really needed to hear, I feel as though I have grown over the last week and I am more determined to make my dreams come true. I actually asked for a promotion today. I'm not going to worry about the outcome, I am just so pleased that I believed enough in myself to ask. I look forward to meeting with you again when I am ready for another growth spurt."

"You were spot on with so many things that you said and I'm still processing it all! I came home and started a journal to write down my feelings and to say what I'm grateful for every day! I felt a whole lot lighter as soon as I left you today and can see that I can have the future I've always dreamt of with a bit of inner soul searching and learning to love myself first! My mind was absolutely blown when you mentioned my overseas dream... Nominating the country I've dreamt about since a small child.. You truely are gifted and I can't wait to visit you on a regular basis ..."

"Thank you for sharing your gift with me, I was amazed at how accurate you were. You have such a warm and comforting manner; I am already thinking about booking a second reading."

"Coming in to see you I was extremely nervous... the furthest thing from my mind was my mother, your accuracy around her and our relationship completely blew me away as only close family and friends know. In 12 months time I will come and see you again to explore more. You have given me the confidence to keep moving forward in my own personal fulfillment."

"What can I say? Thank you seems so trite, considering you seem to have peered deep into my soul. Lucy and I have known each other for a number of years but lived our lives part for most of that time. I asked Lucy to read for me as I was going through a particularly difficult spell in my life. Lucy's reading has helped me see a way through my situation and provided guidance as to how I could perhaps deal with some of the more trying elements that were weighing me down. Lucy's intuition is 'bob on' and moreover there is no way Lucy could have known about issues facing me. Lucy has a rare gift, if you are searching for answers, either personally or from a business perspective, Lucy really can help, her truth and kindness know no bounds and I am looking forward to seeing where my next reading takes me."

"Lucy was fantastic and I felt very comfortable with her. Lucy didn't need to ask many questions and she was spot on, one of the best readings I've had. I've referred friends and family and they all agree Lucy's abilities are amazing. I will definitely be back to visit again and will be booking in for a longer reading - 30 minutes passed so quickly!"

"I just wanted to say thank you for my reading earlier this week. You have a beautiful, calm and gentle way of delivering the information that needs to get to the people you see. I felt so comfortable and calm in your presence and I couldn't believe how accurate your information was. I went in feeling lost and confused and came out feeling inspired, clear thinking and looking forward to the next step forward. After going through a very hard period in my life I just didn't know which way to turn or which decision to make and now after seeing you I feel excited about the future and now know what I need to do. Everything you said was absolutely spot on. You have helped me so much, thank you, what you do is amazing."

Lightning Source UK Ltd.
Milton Keynes UK
UKOW04f1020201215
264982UK00009B/49/P